P9-DWJ-306

AHEAD OF OUR TIME

Chapel Hill's First Nightingales

**UNC Chapel Hill School of Nursing
Class of 1955**

Arlene Morgan Thurstone
Bette Leon Davis
Donna Blair Booe
Geraldine Snider Laport
Gloria Huss Peele
Gwenlyn Huss Butler
Janet Merritt Littlejohn
Joy Smith Burton
Louise Norwood Thomas
Martha Yount Cline
Mary Anderson Leggette
Pat Colvard Johnson
Ramelle Hylton Starnes
Sally Winn Nicholson
Sara Blaylock Flynn
Virginia Edwards Coupe

Edited by Nancy D. Lamontagne

Copyright © 2014 by 1955 Nightingales Corporation
All rights reserved.
ISBN: 0692320059
ISBN-13: 9780692320051
Library of Congress Control Number: 2014922033
Published by 1955 Nightingales Corporation, Alexandria, Virginia

*In memory of Elizabeth Louanna Kemble (1906–1981),
dean of the University of North Carolina at Chapel
Hill School of Nursing from 1950 to 1968.*

Acknowledgements

Members of the class of 1955 are deeply grateful to the following people for their help in writing this book: Anne Aldridge Webb, the assistant dean of advancement at the UNC Chapel Hill School of Nursing, who encouraged and guided our writing process; each classmate, whose friendship began in 1951 and continues; the original School of Nursing faculty, as well as the deans and faculty who followed Dean Kemble and continue to advance nursing education, research, and expand roles in nursing; and Nancy D. Lamontagne, who turned our stories into a historical narrative.

Table of Contents

Introduction

A four-year program in baccalaureate nursing education was brand new in North Carolina in 1951, when twenty-seven young women stepped on campus to begin their studies as part of the first class of the University of North Carolina (UNC) School of Nursing in Chapel Hill.

Pioneers at the age of eighteen, they were also the first full class of freshman women at the university. This first class changed the way nurses would be educated in the state and secured a stronger place for women at UNC Chapel Hill.

The University of North Carolina School of Nursing was established in 1950 through the advocacy of the state's Good Health Program, as part of the North Carolina General Assembly's goal to create a complete health education campus in Chapel Hill.

University administration hired founding dean Elizabeth L. Kemble to direct the new school. A prominent nurse leader with an impressive educational background and a strong personality, she had the necessary skills to advocate for the School of Nursing throughout North Carolina, hire faculty, and recruit the first students. She and her faculty were quite renowned nationally in the field, and the school's first class was a handpicked group of young women ready to become UNC's first nurses.

Of the women who entered in 1951, seventeen finished the program. After graduation, these nurses practiced in the postwar economy at a time when segregation was still commonplace and the women's movement had yet to take place.

Holding the rare bachelor of science in nursing degree placed them in leadership positions early in their careers, whether they were ready or not. Many of them had strong military connections that began with having fathers or other family members who served in World War II and in the Korean War. For some members of the class of 1955, their own career paths, or those of their husbands, further developed those military connections. The skills and leadership of this first class made a difference in care and policy in North Carolina, around the country, and in several other parts of the world.

Six decades have passed since the UNC School of Nursing enrolled the first class. The charter members who initially appear in this story as young girls in the early 1950s have become grandmothers, some even great-grandmothers. Changes have been vast, yet there is one thing that prevails and continues undaunted: their intrinsic value for healing, compassion, empathy, and service.

Prologue: Looking Back after Fifty Years

June 6, 2005, was a glorious and sunny day. It was the 211th gradu-ation day for the University of North Carolina at Chapel Hill. In cap and gown, our pioneering nursing class of 1955 led the procession into Kenan Stadium in celebration of UNC's class of 1955's fiftieth reunion.

This time, like at all our other gatherings, we reminisced about the fun times and the challenges that were uniquely ours as the first class of nurses at UNC Chapel Hill.

With nostalgia, we remembered the mob of boys outside our dorm yelling "throw panties," and how later we had to adjust to the sound of gurneys rolling by our rooms as we slept in temporary quarters in pa-tients' rooms at the brand-new North Carolina Memorial Hospital. We recalled our great respect for Dean Kemble as she guided us in what it meant to be a nurse and our fear at having to ask her permission to get married while still in school.

Looking back, we realize that we were witnessing important changes in patient care and were helping to not just change nursing education, but also adjust the views some had of nurses.

Of the graduates who began in 1951, only two were not with us to celebrate fifty years. Arlene Morgan Thurstone could not attend, and, sadly, Virginia Edwards Coupe had died in January 1995. The next five years passed quickly, and it was soon time to celebrate our fifty-fifth class reunion. This time the bell tolled for Sara Blaylock Flynn, who lost a valiant battle with cancer in October 2008.

As time and events marched on, the loss of our classmates sparked a call to action. Our individual and collective reminiscences coalesced into a group desire to write about our class and to document our later journeys.

Even though we have had stops, starts, and pauses in our progress of this book, our memories have kept us laughing and going on, no matter what happened. It is with a chuckle about all the old times, upheavals and all, then and now, that kept us saying that we *shall* finish this chronicle.

Class of 1955
School of Nursing
University of North Carolina, Chapel Hill

1

A Pioneering New School Recruits Its First Class

The first four faculty members for the School of Nursing were (from left) Alice Gifford, Dean Kemble, Ruth Dalrymple, and Ruth Boyles.

By the mid-1940s, a push began for a School of Nursing to be included in what would be a new concept in healing arts for meeting the health needs of North Carolina—a UNC Division of Health Affairs. Under the umbrella of this division, a new School of Nursing and a new School of Dentistry would join the already established Schools of Medicine, Pharmacy, and Public Health. Public support garnered by the state's Good Health campaign and legislative appropriations in the mid- and late-1940s made the UNC Health Affairs Division and its new School of Nursing a reality. Dr. Henry Toole Clark Jr. headed this new division and appointed Dr. Elizabeth Kemble as dean.[1]

Dean Kemble arrived for full-time work on August 1, 1950. Her doctoral-level education and reputation as a progressive thinker attracted superbly qualified nursing faculty. To recruit and admit students to the first class, Dean Kemble and faculty members Alice Gifford, Ruth Dalrymple, and Ruth Boyles spread the news about the School's opening in the fall of 1951. They had the foresight and dedication to provide a collegiate nursing degree, which was quite different from the traditional three-year hospital training that most nurses received at this time.

In 1949, only 114 collegiate schools of nursing were included in the 11,193 state-accredited schools of nursing in the United States and its territories. Only 61 of the collegiate schools conferred a bachelor's degree on every graduate, with 45 offering the choice of a degree or diploma program, and 8 offered diploma programs only.[2]

In recruiting the first class, Dean Kemble and the faculty members sent a letter to 737 North Carolina high school

Dr. Elizabeth Kemble

principals, visited high schools, and publicized the four-year collegiate program at UNC in newspaper articles and radio announcements around the state. They emphasized that students would receive professional nursing training and a broad college education. Although potential for admission to the program was equal, opportunity was not. In 1951 segregation still existed, and it would not be until the 1960s that students of diversity in race or sex would receive degrees from the School of Nursing.

Everyone who would become a member of the School of Nursing's first class had planned to attend college. Several of them had applied to Women's College in Greensboro, North Carolina, (now the University of North Carolina at Greensboro) and after two years there they planned to transfer to the School of Nursing at Duke University, where in three more years they could obtain a baccalaureate nursing degree.

Many of the students learned about the new School of Nursing from their fathers. For example, Mary Anderson had made plans to enter Women's College and then transfer to Duke University after two years. "My father read of the new School of Nursing at UNC in *The Durham Sun* in June, 1951. It carried an encouraging photograph captioned 'School of Nursing Going Up.' He suggested that I apply and consider the program there, where I could graduate in four years." Mary had an older brother already in Chapel Hill. She applied to the school, and Mrs. Gifford visited their home. "We all liked the prospect of the new school and the privilege and responsibility of being the first class."

Some of the students, such as Donna Blair, had been exposed to nursing since a young age. Her mother had been a nursing student at Case Western Reserve University in Ohio, and her father graduated from dental school at the University of Pittsburgh.

"Dad set up his practice in Ohio during the depression when the country was just beginning to surface from dire circumstances, and often dental visits were paid for with a chicken or some tasty home-made pickles, or better yet, pie. Mother made all the dental appointments, assisted Dad at the chair, kept the books, and 'mothered' my sister and me with all the treasures of having a nurturing mother."

After World War II was declared, Donna's mother became head of a Red Cross Chapter. "I went to meetings with her, and ladies were knitting socks, scarves, and little helmet-liner caps," Donna recalls. "I diligently rolled bandages and secured them with a little pin. I remember drawing a large red cross on a piece of folded white paper and making my own Red Cross cap. Dad was called into the Army Air Corps when I was in the second grade, and any thought of nursing was dormant until I began my senior year in high school."

Donna planned to attend Emory University in Atlanta for a nursing degree. "I was spending the summer after my senior year with my grandmother in Florida, and in midsummer my dad called long distance to tell me about a fortuitous article he had read in the *Winston-Salem Journal* and the *Sentinel*," she says. "It detailed a new baccalaureate nursing program that was being initiated at UNC Chapel Hill. Dad called Dean Kemble. I came home, and then Mother and I drove to Chapel Hill to meet with Ruth Boyles, Alice Gifford, and Dean Kemble. I was enrolled that very day. How fortunate for me to be in that particular place at that particular time, for it has shaped my entire life."

Pat Colvard had been accepted at Sweet Briar College in Virginia, where she planned to take pre-nursing courses. "I read about UNC's new program in the Durham newspaper, and my father was exceedingly happy to send me there instead. He could see that the UNC School of Nursing would provide me with not only a college education, but also a way to earn a living. Although I would have taken pre-nursing courses at Sweet Briar College, this was a quicker and less expensive way to that goal."

Bette Davis knew that she was destined to be a nurse. "My earliest memories include wearing my mom's nursing cap and playing the nurse in doctor-nurse-patient games. Mom was a registered nurse with the US Department of Interior, Indian Service, and working in Concho, Oklahoma, when I was born. Her marriage to my father, an army sergeant stationed at Fort Reno, Oklahoma, ended in divorce. When I was two years old, my mother returned to her ancestral home in Morganton, North Carolina, to be near my grandmother." After a short stay there, they moved to Charlotte, where Bette's mother worked at Mercy Hospital, until she married another army staff sergeant she had known while in Oklahoma. After that Bette lived in several states, spending her sophomore year in the large, integrated high school of Junction City, Kansas.

"I became interested in working part time as a nurse's aide after school and on weekends at the Junction City Hospital. Mom, who worked there as a substitute supervisor, helped me get employed and taught me some basics of aides' duties. The rest I learned from the nursing staff. I particularly remember a young nurse who had recently graduated from the University of Michigan School of Nursing with a BSN. The idea of an integrated collegiate BSN degree was planted. I loved working with her and the patients."

After one year in Kansas, it was back to North Carolina for her junior and senior years at Morganton High School. "I was back with friends I had known since early childhood." Mrs. Gifford visited her high school just before graduation while Bette and her classmate Arlene were touring Washington, DC, on a senior class trip. "She spoke with our homeroom teacher, who later informed us about the nursing program opening in the fall," Bette says.

Arlene Morgan had been accepted to a five-year degree program at the University of Virginia School of Nursing. Bette was accepted at

Mars Hill Junior College, and after completing course work there, she planned to attend Duke University. "Within a week of hearing about Chapel Hill, I drove there with Arlene and her mother for interviews with Dean Kemble, Ms. Boyles, and Mrs. Gifford," Bette recalls. "This was the beginning of the application process, and everything changed when we received our letters of acceptance."

Virginia Edwards read about the new nursing program in the Durham newspaper, according to her sister and daughter. She was awarded a scholarship from the Business Women's Club of Durham, North Carolina, based on her high school studies. Their whole family felt honored that Ginny was admitted to the School of Nursing.

In high school, Sara Blaylock's goal was to leave her hometown of New Bern, North Carolina. Her uncle, who was in the military, had traveled the world and gave Sara firsthand information about what life was like in other places. Sara recognized that a qualified nurse could get a job most anywhere in the world, and she decided on the UNC School of Nursing as the place that would give her the nursing education that could take her to new places where she could help people.

Twin sisters Gloria and Gwen Huss were enrolled at Women's College in Greensboro and had even paid their room rent. Gloria planned on four years there, after which she would transfer to Duke's nursing program, for a total of seven years. After Ms. Boyles visited their home in Thomasville, four years sounded much better to Gloria, and Gwen decided to join her, switching from a business major. Interviews followed, and Ms. Boyles announced that it would be very nice to have twins in the first class.

Ramelle "Rae" Hylton and Geraldine "Geri" Snider had known each other since eighth grade and had signed up to be roommates at Woman's College in Greensboro. "During my senior year in high school, my chemistry teacher took a group of us to tour Chapel Hill and the chemistry labs," Rae says. "I fell in love with the campus and planned to enroll as soon as I could, but women could not enroll until their junior year." Rae's friends and high school classmates Gloria and Gwen told her that the new School of Nursing was recruiting students.

Geri says that during the summer after graduating from high school, Rae called her to tell her about the School of Nursing opening at Carolina. Rae said, "Let's apply," and so they did. "August 27, 1951, set the course for the rest of my life," Geri says. "That was the date of my letter of acceptance from Elizabeth L. Kemble, dean of the School of Nursing at the University of North Carolina at Chapel Hill. I had no way of guessing all that would happen in the years ahead, but I was thrilled with the possibilities jumping around in my head. I was even happier because I would be rooming with Rae, my best friend from the eighth grade, when my family lived in High Point before moving to Fayetteville."

Janet Merritt lived in Chapel Hill. This university town exposed her to caring for others at a young age. "It is a unique place with a village of families, just like other small towns, but also a university with a population of students, predominantly transient, who spend their years in education there."

Dr. Lloyd was the only doctor in Chapel Hill when Janet was growing up. Babies were born at home, and he always brought one of the local ladies to assist in delivering a baby. Otherwise, treating sick and bedridden patients was primarily the responsibility of family and neighbors. "I learned early in life about care for the ailing and infirm as I accompanied my mother or grandmother on visits," Janet says.

"Usually, we took food prepared for the entire family, and we would bathe, feed, and position some of the people, especially those who had cancer or who had suffered a stroke. Perhaps this was an introduction to nursing for me, as I enjoyed being able to help wash faces and hands or feed and offer water to persons who could not do so for themselves. The elderly were filled with gratitude, and the families very grateful for palliative care we could offer."

School had always been important for Janet, but became even more so in high school, as she set her sights on college. "I had no idea what path I would choose, so I equipped myself for different choices. My science courses went well, and one of my teachers suggested a medical career."

During Janet's senior year, she was elected secretary of the student government council, the governing body of her high school. This led to her being chosen as a delegate for North Carolina Girls' State. The meeting was held at Woman's College in Greensboro. "I was so impressed with the school. I tentatively decided to attend college there," she says. "This was, however, before I knew about the new nursing program at UNC."

Janet's school bus stop was a short walk from her house, and a lady often gave her a ride. "She introduced herself as Elizabeth, and through our conversation I assumed she was a professor," recalls Janet. On one occasion she asked Janet about her plans after graduation and then proceeded to talk about the new baccalaureate nursing program at UNC, encouraging Janet to consider it as an option.

"I asked if she could arrange an application for me from the university," Janet says. "It arrived two days later in the mail, along with a time for an interview. I immediately returned the application. When I walked into the room for my interview, I recognized the warm smile and twinkling eyes as I was introduced to 'my friend,' Dean Elizabeth Kemble. What a surprise! A lively conversation followed, as she admitted I had already had several 'interviews.' She had received the required papers needed for admission, and I would receive a formal letter soon from the university to welcome me as a member of the freshman class of the School of Nursing. I was overjoyed to be accepted into this new pioneer nursing program."

Louise Norwood had attended Mars Hill Junior College for two years. When she heard about the new nursing school, she was in the process of transferring to Greensboro to obtain a four-year degree. "With a degree in hand, I planned to then enter nursing school," she recalls. "I received a letter from UNC about the new program and arranged an interview with Dean Kemble and Mrs. Gifford. I was happy I could achieve my goal of a college degree and nursing education in four years."

At just three years old, Joy Smith knew that she was on her way to a very successful nursing career when she nursed her doll back to health. Joy had just gotten over the intestinal flu when all her dolls became sick. "The famous Dy-Dee doll was my favorite patient. Her rubber ears could be cleaned with a cotton swab. She had her own baby-sized bottle and drank loads of water, which meant her diaper had to be changed often. She was the first patient to recover. I know because of all the fluids (water) she drank."

Joy's choice of a nursing career was later influenced by a very old friend of their family, "Ms. Ann"—Ann Ashe, RN—a retired nurse who took care of Joy and her brother and sister when her parents traveled or were ill. "I began to love and adore her. She told me many stories of her nursing years and experiences."

Joy had applied to Baptist Hospital Nursing School in Winston-Salem and had even taken admission exams. But early in the spring of 1951, her parents were returning from a business trip in Raleigh, when they just happened to turn on the car radio and heard Dean Kemble making a compelling speech about the new BSN degree that could be obtained through a four-year nursing program in Chapel Hill.

"My daddy whipped the car around in the highway and headed for 'The Hill,'" Joy says. "They secured a hurried appointment with the dean, whose office at this time was in a trailer. Dean Kemble then sent a letter to me asking me to meet with her the following week in Chapel Hill. That was the beginning of the rest of my life."

Winnie Williams first learned of the opening of the UNC School of Nursing from her dentist while at an appointment in July of 1951. "My original plan was two years of pre-nursing course work at Woman's College, and then three years at the Duke University School of Nursing. I remember little of the interviewing or testing process for admission, but I do remember some of the fear I had of going to Carolina. After all, it was a boy's school with no freshman girls except for a few local residents or those in the pharmacy school. My parents and I were reassured by a Carolina graduate, who said that the school could be what you made of it."

Sally Winn did not pretend to be a nurse as a child, nor was she interested in caring for children. "The career I fantasized about was airline stewardess," she recalls. "I dreamed of flying. From the earliest time I remember thinking of a future, I *knew* that I would go to college. I expected that I would have a career. This was not a general expectation for young people of my family or community, who expected that children would grow up to carry on the family occupation of farming."

When Sally tried out the idea of nursing, she received mixed responses. "My chemistry teacher advised college. A cousin, who was the daughter of a physician, was supportive of nursing. She had wanted to be a nurse, but that was forbidden—not something "nice" girls did in the early nineteen hundreds. My aunt, who was my second mother, thought it was not a bad idea. Tuition for nursing school was small, and we could find the money. Another aunt laughed at the idea. 'You can't be a nurse,' she said. 'You're too lazy!' That did it. My stubborn Welsh streak was engaged. I would be a nurse. I would show her."

Sally began researching nursing programs and was somewhat disenchanted until reading a newspaper article about the UNC program. "I sent in my application, along with a scholarship application. As the daughter of a disabled veteran attending a state-supported school, I was eligible for a full scholarship."

A cousin drove Sally to Chapel Hill for interviews. "She also introduced me to the dean of the medical school, Dr. Berryhill, who was a distant relative. I knew so little about the academic world that I thought that the title "doctor" meant that Dr. Kemble was a physician. I received notice of acceptance to the school during the spring of 1951. In July, I learned that I had won a scholarship. The period between these two events was a somewhat anxious one. I had told everyone that I was going to Carolina, but without the scholarship, this would have been impossible."

Martha Yount had a friend at UNC who told her there would be a new School of Nursing opening there in 1951. "The nursing school would offer a college degree on a college campus. My first interview with Dean Kemble was scheduled for a very snowy day with icy roads, 160 miles from Hickory, North Carolina. My older brothers encouraged my dad to let me drive despite the weather, but only after giving me many driving instructions."

When Martha arrived in Chapel Hill, Miller Hall, the temporary home of the School of Nursing, was closed. "They had tried to reach me earlier, but I had already left. This was before the days of cell phones," she recalls. "This was a disappointment, but being young and having other plans for the weekend, everything turned out okay. I returned for another appointment on another Chapel Hill weekend. After my interview with the dean and nursing school staff, I went to my mailbox every day to see if the anticipated letter had arrived. The day of its arrival in February was a happy day."

The twenty-seven students recruited to be in the first School of Nursing class came from all over North Carolina, and a few were from other states.

Below is a list of the first seventeen graduates with their hometowns:

Arlene Morgan Thurstone, Morganton, NC
Bette Leon Davis, Morganton, NC
Donna Blair Booe, Winston-Salem, NC
Geraldine "Geri" Snider Laport, Fayetteville, NC
Gloria Huss Peele, Thomasville, NC
Gwenlyn Huss Butler, Thomasville, NC
Janet Merritt Littlejohn, Chapel Hill, NC
Joy Smith Burton, Charlotte, NC
Louise Norwood Thomas, Winston-Salem, NC
Martha Yount Cline, Hickory, NC
Mary Anderson Leggette, Durham, NC
Patsy "Pat" Colvard Johnson, Durham, NC
Ramelle "Rae" Hylton Starnes, High Point, NC
Sally Winn Nicholson, Henderson, NC
Sara Blaylock Flynn, New Bern, NC
Virginia Edwards Coupe, Durham, NC
Winnie Williams Cotton, Fayetteville, NC

---

[1] Gayle Lane Fitzgerald. (1991). *The School of Nursing at the University of North Carolina in Chapel Hill and the Pioneers Who Built It.*

[2] National Committee for the Improvement of Nursing Services. (1950). Nursing Schools at the Mid-Century.

2

Freshman Year

Twenty-seven girls arrived on campus on September 14, 1951, a perfectly beautiful autumn day. Traveling from all directions—from the mountains to the coast and from north and south parts of the state—they converged on Chapel Hill. Two members of the class came from out of state, and one drove only a few miles from home, thus having the distinction of being a "town" girl. Community newspaper articles announced the "history-making class."

This friendly bunch quickly connected with each other.

Sally, Rae, Pat, and Geri with Dean Kemble in front of Miller Hall, the home of the School of Nursing until the fall of 1952.

They had much in common as children of the 1930s who were white, female, and around eighteen years old. They dressed similarly, wearing skirts, loafers with white bobby socks, and either a shirt or short-sleeve sweater with a Peter Pan collar or a small square scarf tied at the neck. Most of them had medium-short hair, and several were high school valedictorians or salutatorians.

For their freshman year, Smith Dormitory was home. It was conveniently located on the old campus near class buildings and the downtown area. The classic colonial red-brick building had large windowpanes with wavy distortions and imperfections that attested to their age. The small dormitory housed only fifty-eight girls, twenty-seven of whom were the new nursing students, and the rest junior and senior coeds in various majors.

"We got to know everyone living there," Bette says. "We are the only class of nursing students to live on campus as freshmen for an entire year. This socialization shaped our simultaneous identification as coed students and nursing students, loyal to both classifications without conflict."

Donna recalls that the weather was crisp, yet warm in the sunshine, on the day she and her mother drove from Winston-Salem to Chapel Hill. "My belongings were packed in suitcases and boxes, but what I remember most were my burnt-orange and chartreuse cashmere sweater sets, Tangee orange lipstick, and bottle of Tigress spray cologne. We arrived at Smith Dormitory and were met by Mrs. Sedalia Gold, the housemother. She was stately and grandmotherly. She wore sensible shoes, had softly powdered skin, and graciously escorted us to my room."

As a native of Chapel Hill, Janet had spent many years walking by the ivy-covered walls of the big buildings on campus, stopping by the Old Well for a sip of cool water, and gathering with friends at the Bell Tower or at a football game. She was now part of the university with which she had grown up. "I could have found myself in any area of the United States, but here I was unloading boxes and clothes three miles away from my home. The buildings I had walked by now had names—they were my classrooms—and the campus seemed to be another world as I found my way around and moved to Smith Dormitory. I enjoyed the hustle and bustle, meeting everyone, talking, and laughing as we made our many trips back and forth to the car."

Bette roomed with her high school classmate Arlene. "Already knowing someone helped my transition to college," Bette says. "We had an end suite tucked under the eaves of the roof on the third floor. One side of the suite had a study alcove containing two big desks beneath large double windows. From here I had a beautiful view of campus buildings, lawn, and trees—an easy distraction from studying too. A door led to a small, cozy, but spacious bedroom, where we each had a twin bed, chest, closet, and window. The separate study and sleeping areas proved invaluable for late and all-night study sessions."

Rae recalls her excitement at meeting the first class of nursing students at Smith Dorm and beginning many wonderful, lasting relationships. "I have often wished that every freshman nursing student could have the experience of living in Smith Dorm and of being centrally located on campus with other coeds," she says. "We felt such a part of the greater university, and the interaction with the coeds was beneficial for us and for them."

Winnie recalls that there were girls everywhere in the dorm. "I had been used to a more solitary environment—raised on a farm as an only child until fourteen years of age," she says. Winnie's roommate, Jeanne, had two years of previous college experience and thus was more familiar with the college atmosphere than we were. "She pointed me in the right direction many times that freshman year," Winnie says.

For Bette, adjustments and surprises began early, on the first day to be exact. "I loaned a nickel to a classmate, and that prompted unsolicited advice from another classmate on not lending money," she says. "However, the loan was repaid."

"Gwen and I came to Chapel Hill very naïve, I believe," says Gloria. "We were excited and thrilled to be involved with the college and the new nursing program. We roomed together the first year, probably for moral support as much as anything. Everyone was excited and anxious to meet other classmates and settle in at Smith Dorm."

Janet enjoyed an immediate friendship with her roommate, Pat Corbett. "Her home was Swansboro, North Carolina—her mother a nurse, and her father a doctor. She had a sister who was already a senior at UNC. Pat seemed perfectly suited for this new nursing program. Our room was located directly adjacent to the fire escape, which could come in handy at any given moment."

Sara and Louise in Smith Dorm.

There was one wall phone and a community bathroom for the floor. "Everyone was supposed to take a turn answering the telephone and call out a name to accept (or reject) the phone call," recalls Janet. "Even though the phone would sometimes ring many times before it was answered, we

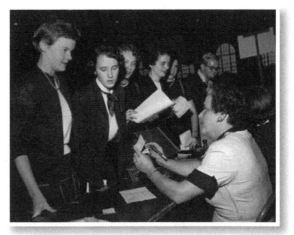

Arlene, Janet, Pat, and Mary register for classes.

never seemed to miss that really important phone call from home. There was a touch of homesickness within us all."

On move-in day, Donna met Sara and Louise, who had attended other colleges previously. "Coincidentally, Brantley Booe, whom I was dating, was a junior at North Carolina State in Raleigh and told me that Louise had been his first girlfriend in the third or fourth grade. I could see why. She looked like a beautiful little doll with big brown eyes and curly dark hair," Donna recalls.

Louise had just come from Mars Hill College, where smoking, drinking, and dancing were not allowed. "My first 'real world' jolt came upon entering my assigned room on the third floor of Smith Dorm," Louise recalls. "My roommate, Sara, had already arrived, and apparently was out meeting others. She had, however, left evidence of previous college life—cigarettes, an ashtray, and a picture of a real sailor. Sara was great, and we got along well, but I'm sure I was a pain in many ways."

Sara was from New Bern, North Carolina, on the coast. Donna says that Sara was her idea of total sophistication, especially when she smoked. "When she inhaled and exhaled, each eyelash-fringed blink of the eyes was like a movie star, lashes falling slowly and opening with a sweep that one could not ignore. I was the youngest in the class and had never smoked. However, watching Sara prompted me to buy my first pack of filtered Winston cigarettes. It was not a good idea. Not only were my eyelashes not long enough to do that sexy sweeping action, but when I tried to inhale, I coughed and got so dizzy that I had to brush my teeth for ten minutes to mask the taste and then fell into my bed for the rest of the afternoon. I never tried it again—the glamour remained Sara's domain."

Microwave ovens and mini refrigerators did not exist, so the nursing students purchased meals. Mary recalls eating at the Carolina

Coffee Shop and driving to The Pines Restaurant as a special treat. After trying the cafeteria in Lenoir Hall for about a month, Bette usually ate at NC Cafeteria, a restaurant located on Franklin Street. "Having limited snacks available and a great deal of walking kept me thin."

A driveway behind Smith Dorm ended in midblock and became an alley-like walkway to Franklin Street, the main drag. "Just as you got to the alley, the School of Public Health was housed on the right in an old wooden building," Donna says. "Directly across the alley was a favorite restaurant, The Porthole. It evoked a feeling of a vacation or someplace foreign. No doubt it got its name from the real ship's porthole mounted in the entrance door."

"Nurses Given NIX on Hostess Jobs"

The nursing students made the local newspaper quite a few times that first year, and the stories were not always good. One headline read "Nurses Given NIX on Hostess Jobs," referring to Dean Kemble putting a stop to six of them entertaining and dancing with students in one of the rooms of the campus cafeteria. "We learned an important lesson: We were not here to entertain the boys," recalls Bette. Donna recounts the experience:

> The large and centrally located Lenoir Hall cafeteria was a great place for lunch. Since classes were close by, we could stay there until the last minute and still make it to class on time (punctuality was a prominent virtue in my home). The truth is, the cafeteria had good food and plenty of boys. Bette, Arlene, Virginia, Sara, Janet, and I were "regulars." In fact, we were so regular that the cafeteria manager thought we knew everyone who had ever sat near us.

The Pine Room, complete with jukebox, was on the downstairs level of Lenoir Hall. The Pine Room manager might have been thinking of selling more Cokes, hot dogs, and fries when he approached us with a wonderful offer: If we would talk and dance with boys in the Pine Room, we could eat lunch free in the cafeteria. Well, we didn't take long to consider, because we all liked to dance and to eat for free. Virginia loved to dance so much that she said she would only marry a boy who could dance. She ended up marrying an American Airlines pilot, who I'm certain was quite a dancer.

Things went well in the Pine Room for a few afternoons. More boys came to dance, and we ate desserts and whatever we wanted for lunch. That is, until an article appeared in the local paper. The next thing I know, I'm sitting in Dean Kemble's office with Bette, facing a radically different kind of music.

The headline of the article said in bold print, "Nurses Given NIX on Hostess Jobs." This was the first I had heard of the article. Dean Kemble questioned us, and we each gave our rationale for our naïve and apparent lapse of judgment. When my turn came, I sat up straight and said, "I thought it would save my folks money." Mother later called to tell me that the dean phoned her to recount the meeting and was laughing when she finished the tale.

The Panty Raid

The infamous "panty raid" episode made it clear to the nursing students that most of the undergraduates were aware of their presence in Smith Dormitory. Donna recounts the episode that none of them will forget:

> Our evening study hours required us to stay in the dorm from 7:00 to 10:00 p.m. One night Virginia and I heard a commotion. To see what was happening, we ran from our room on the second floor in the back of the dorm to the hall bath in the front of the building. When we opened the window, we were stunned to see a surging mass of humanity advancing on the front lawn. A surreal, boisterous mob of boys was running shoulder-to-shoulder and hollering "throw panties." While shocking, it *was* funny. We were laughing so much that I decided to heighten our entertainment by heaving a roll of toilet paper out the window, laughing as it streamed into the crowd with a long-tailed flourish. Instantly, the noise level picked up, and the energy escalated to the point that I felt an internal alarm. Out of fear that someone would try to break in the door or windows on the first floor, I raced down the stairs two at a time and started checking the locks, when I ran into Mrs. Gold. I felt safer with her, and together we checked the remainder of the doors and windows on the first floor. I remained at her side until the "raid" finally subsided.
>
> The next day I had my second appointment at the dean's request. I really felt guilty and tried to justify my behavior by rationalizing that I just threw toilet paper, certainly not panties! Never, ever panties! I rationalized that toilet paper was just like confetti at a parade.
>
> The solemn meeting began. There were no smiles. Dean Kemble, with her precise diction, said something to the effect of, "I've called you in to talk about

the events of last night." I replied, "Yes, ma'am." Ray Jeffries, assistant to the dean of student affairs, was in the crowd and had recognized me. Even though we could not be seen because the lights were out in the bathroom, he had recognized my laugh. I proceeded to tell Dean Kemble I was with Mrs. Gold, and together we were locking windows and doors. She must have called Mrs. Gold, who was my "golden" witness to that *later* part of the night, for I wasn't summoned again.

Rules and Regulations

Mary recalls that as young women on a major university campus, discipline was imposed on them. There were four pages of restrictive regulations for freshmen in the School of Nursing, including rules for quiet hours and guests.[3] "In the 1980s, I had children in school in Chapel Hill, one in the School of Nursing," she says. "My experience and hers contrast the decades of the fifties and the eighties."

Janet remembers that Mrs. Gold kept a very close watch over the nursing students. Even holding hands with a date made her raise an eyebrow. She had quite a few rules, but they all aligned with her expectation of them to be ladies.

Each time they left the dorm during evening hours, they were required to sign an in/out card on which they noted the time out, destination, companion, and the time back in. Their curfew was 11:00 p.m. during the week and midnight on Saturday and Sunday, and mandatory study hours lasted from 7:00 to 10:00 p.m. each weeknight.

"We often spent our designated free time from 10:00 to 11:00 p.m. each weeknight getting a snack at the Scuttlebutt," Janet says. Winnie recalls the fun they had slipping out to the Scuttlebutt in blue jeans or in rolled up pajama bottoms, covered with raincoats, after closed study. The Scuttlebutt was on the corner of Cameron Avenue and South Columbia Street.

If any rules were broken, the nursing students would appear before the Women's Honor Council to learn their penalty. The Women's Honor Council was the highest women's judiciary body on campus and had original jurisdiction in all cases involving violations of honor and campus codes. It was composed of three juniors, five seniors, one graduate student, and one woman elected at large. The honor court was led by the chairman, who was appointed by the student body president, and selected students made up the remaining council. No student wanted to receive a summons to appear before this group for judgment.

A. MAJOR RULES

1. Closing Hours: Each coed must be in her dormitory:*
   Monday through Thursday---11:00 P. M.
   Friday and Saturday---12:00 P. M.
   Sunday---11:30 P. M.

If late, a girl is to report herself to the House President. She will be brought before the House Council for appropriate action. Punishment will probably be one night's probation up to the first ten minutes, with one night added for every ten minutes afterward. (A House Council warning will be given for the first offense to girls in their first quarter of residence at the University.) Probation means remaining in the residence section of the dormitory from 8 p.m. until 5 a.m. signing in with the House President at 8.

If late, and the dormitory is closed, a girl is to be let in by some member of the dormitory administration. If a girl returns to Chapel Hill during the hours when the dormitory is closed, she is to return immediately to the dormitory. Under no circumstances is she to linger in Chapel Hill or immediate vicinity.

Girls are expected to observe closing hours when returning from weekend absences or vacations. Reasonable exceptions to this rule must be approved by the House President. Girls coming in late for any reason must telephone or telegraph the dormitory administration before dormitory closing hours. Legitimate causes for lateness will be evaluated by the House Councils.

Gloria and Gwen experienced the honor council after coming in late one Sunday night. "It was almost like being in a court session," Gloria recalls. "We did not know if we would be dismissed from college or not. Our continuing in the nursing program was on the line. I cannot remember our punishment, but I do know we were never late again."

Janet learned just how seriously the rules were enforced when she returned from Thanksgiving holiday. "I was shocked to receive a summons from the honor council because I failed to properly sign out for the holiday," she recalls. "In our handbook, if you left town (which all my classmates did), you were required to be signed out 'home.' Chapel Hill *was* my home, so I simply left campus and did not sign out. Obviously, this was a first for the council, so after my explanation and their deliberation, I was given a reprimand and was advised to always sign out in the future. This was a rule that I never forgot."

The Carolina Social Scene

Although they had many rules, Mrs. Gold wanted them to meet other students—mostly male freshmen and sophomores. So on Sundays, they attended tea parties and social gatherings in the parlor of Smith Dorm. "Refreshments, music, dancing, and boys who were eager to meet the freshman girls provided fun as well as future dates," Bette says. "On these occasions, I stood rather than sat, to avoid a surprised look when I stood after being asked for a dance. I was statuesque at five feet and ten inches, taller than the average boy."

Louise was a well-endowed, beautiful, petite brunette and a shy, strict Baptist who did not dance. "Eventually we convinced her to attend a Sunday event," Bette says. "A small group of us stood at the bottom of the staircase encouraging her to join us. When she was halfway down, one of the male students spotted her and started up the steps to greet her. She turned around and went right back upstairs. The first year was not for the faint of heart."

A formal dance was held in Woollen Gym at the end of orientation week, and blind dates were arranged for anyone needing a date. Two fraternity brothers escorted Sara and Bette to the dance. "Once inside, all I could smell was alcohol on their breaths," Bette recalls. "This was a hugely disappointing first blind date for me. However, the night was saved, as there were other boys without dates with whom to dance."

Their social life was limited to campus, since very few of them owned cars. "The movies, ball games, dances, and The Rendezvous Room were the favorite dating venues," Janet says. "The Rendezvous Room was in the basement of the Graham Memorial building and had a jukebox, snack bar, huge dance floor, and soft lights. This was the big-band era, and even today, when I hear 'Tenderly,' 'Autumn Leaves,' and 'Sentimental Journey,' I think of the evenings we danced in The Rendezvous Room."

"Since I loved to dance, as most of us did, I usually spent Friday evenings dancing in the Rendezvous Room. I also went to the big dance weekend sponsored by the German Club each quarter," Bette says. Representatives from thirteen social fraternities composed the German Club, whose purpose was to select big-name bands for concerts and dances. Girls from other campuses, referred to as "imports," were invited to campus as special dates for these weekends.

"We also enjoyed going to the football and basketball games, Sunday afternoon picnics, and activities such as square dances at the Y Court," Winnie says. Geri remembers admiring the Old Well on the way to class and hanging out in the Y Court in spare minutes between classes and taking a few minutes to admire the beauty of the arboretum.

Janet spent spring break in Swansboro, North Carolina. "Pat and Ginger each invited three friends to visit them there, and Mary and I went as Pat's guests. Dr. Corbett took us down the Inland Waterway on their yacht. We soaked up lots of sun, not realizing how strong it was with the nice cool breeze. Mrs. Corbett served a delicious lunch in the galley. Later we changed clothes for an evening dinner and dancing at Wrightsville Beach. Pat's parents had prearranged dates for each of us—friends of the family from UNC or other colleges. We had lots of fun dancing the shag on the strand. The next day, a group of tired and sunburned girls drove back to Chapel Hill, some sleeping most of the way. What a memorable vacation that was for me, and I will always remember the gracious and thoughtful Dr. and Mrs. Corbett."

Learning Important Lessons

Although it was fun engaging in social events and campus activities, the struggle this first year was the course work. The curriculum for this brand-new program incorporated classes such as English, chemistry, and zoology, which the nursing students took with other university students, as well as nursing classes taught by School of Nursing faculty. Over the years, the nursing curriculum would undergo many changes as the school created courses tailored for nurses and constantly evaluated how to meet the educational needs of an advancing profession.

"Not only were there early morning classes, but we also had lab classes in the afternoons," Janet says. "We accepted this busy schedule and searched the campus for the building for each course. The large campus I had passed through all these years was as confusing to me as it was to everyone else."

Winnie remembers that registering for classes and finding the locations for classes was facilitated by the fact that there were always girls going the same direction.

During the first quarter, Bette discovered that she didn't know how to study or write at the level required by the university, yet she persevered and successfully passed this boot camp. "My struggle and growth had been worth it, preparing me for the second and third quarters," Bette says. "It helped a lot to attend church on Sundays at the Chapel of the Cross and also see Dean Kemble relying on a higher power."

Some of them were not prepared for the rapid review of what they should have learned in high school. Bette was not the only one shocked to see her high school A in English become a C in college, and her A in chemistry turned into a D at UNC. "Anything below seventy was an F at UNC," she says. "At a Christmas party, I discovered that some of my high school classmates who were C students received A's in other colleges."

Geri remembers that chemistry was extremely difficult. "I had taken chemistry in high school, but this seemed like another universe. I studied consistently. Then before each exam I prayed at our Smith Dormitory room window, 'Please, God, please help me pass my chemistry exam tomorrow.' I think these prayers were answered, as I passed organic and inorganic chemistry with anxiety and flying colors."

Sally's high school had no chemistry lab, so her only experiments had been with her chemistry set at home. "How exciting it was to use the equipment to carry out experiments," she recalls. "I was assigned to the test and laboratory sessions taught by Dr. Markham, the course professor. I was an eager little guppy, gulping down new facts, and the only girl in his test section. I had many questions, which must have prolonged the Friday sessions."

Janet remembers being armed with infamous Blue Books and seated at every other desk for chemistry exams, which were scheduled at night. "A time limit was set, and writing feverishly, you simply hoped to finish within the allotted time," she says. "Even if you were in the middle of a sentence or problem, you stopped, signed the honor pledge, 'I have neither given nor received help on this exam,' and handed the Blue Book to the professor. Later, you got it back with a big red letter on it."

One day during chemistry lab, Donna was standing near Pat at the lab table while they all did the same experiment. "All of a sudden Pat grabbed her eye and bolted," Donna says. "I caught her motion out of the corner of my eye, but all I could do was audibly gasp. In a flash, the teaching assistant grabbed her, half carrying her to a shower with a hose mounted in the lab floor. I had never even noticed it before. He held her head back while flushing her eye with a continual stream of water for what seemed like an eternity. To this day I breathe a sigh of relief for his instant and appropriate response."

Pat says that there was a quick ride to the Durham eye hospital and no permanent damage. "The most interesting part was that I did end up dating the nice, cute graduate-student lab instructor named Bill," she recalls.

The nursing professors were eager for them to pass chemistry. "I received a great big hug from Ms. Ruth Boyles when I told her I made a D," Bette says. "I was very happy and relieved to have passed." Some were not as fortunate, repeating the class during the second quarter and failing again. These classmates, as well as some others who either got married or pursued other interests, did not return after the first year.

Mary had graduated from Durham High School, one of the best schools in the state. "Even with an excellent high school background, our courses were challenging," she says. "There were 8:00 a.m. classes after late nights of studying and socializing. I was reprimanded for dozing in that 8:00 a.m. English class, and I learned to drink coffee."

Most of the students did not type or own a typewriter, and handwritten papers were the norm. Winnie says that she certainly did not expect English to be difficult; she expected to make the grades she made in high school. "I had a rude awakening and was somewhat overwhelmed by the material covered in all the courses."

Janet learned the importance of mastering the art of taking notes and keeping them safe. Her desk was in an alcove opposite her room, and she left the note cards for a thousand-word English paper, complete with bibliography, in a big stack contained by a rubber band, poised to be put into typewritten form.

"The next morning, my stack of note cards was missing," Janet recalls. Everyone in the dorm joined the search, but the cards were nowhere to be found. "Evidently, they were taken from my desk during the night. My disbelief quickly turned into frustration and anger, as I had no choice but to head to the library to begin my note taking all over again. The professor graciously granted me an extension of three days when he heard about my dilemma. Fortunately, I had kept a copy of the bibliography and remembered some of my writings, so my term paper was completed by the deadline. To this day, I can still feel the disbelief of it all."

Some of the other girls eventually found money, jewelry, and clothes missing. The suspected culprit did not return the next year, and the thefts abruptly ceased. So, their hunches were likely correct.

Geri says that her roommate, Rae, was not just a wonderful friend, but also had a gift for spelling. "She checked each paper I wrote for English class; otherwise I never would have passed the first three courses we took our first three quarters at UNC."

Zoology 41 and 42 made for a heavy load. "Being familiar with the tricky way exam questions were stated was an advantage," Bette says. "For example, one could memorize all the arteries and veins in a frog, but on an exam, you might be asked to trace the flow of a drop of blood in a specific area, from point A to point B, naming all the arteries and veins en route."

Sally says that, of all the courses, vertebrate zoology was a challenge. "It was known as a weeding-out course for medical school. Dr. Jones taught it and was on the selection committee for the medical school. It was rumored that without at least a B in his course, one could not hope to be selected. I made the only D of my academic career, and was relieved not to have failed."

Janet says that many third-year pre-med and pre-dental students became their allies in zoology, providing helpful hints and special assistance with laboratory assignments. "I remember exposing the three curved tubular canals in a crayfish inner ear, also known as the semicircular canals. This was a tedious process at best, and with each nick in the canal, your grade went lower. So you could go from A to F in a matter of minutes. The pre-med students assisted immensely here—even offering to switch crayfish with us (which would have been wonderful), but with the words of the honor code reverberating in our minds, we opted for status quo. I firmly believe Dr. Jones was sympathetic toward the 'little nurses' when possible. At least there was a smile and an occasional pat on the back for encouragement. I was happy with a C in that course."

Winnie remembers that two of the three invertebrate zoology tests she took were below passing. After the second test, the young man sitting next to her in lecture said, "Whoever made that grade might as well give up." She says that the pre-med student sitting at her lab table would help her focus the microscope and told her what she should be seeing. "I became truly discouraged and called my mom to come for me, telling her there was no way I could pass this course. Needless to say, she refused, and I was left with a bruised ego and too much pride to ask for help, even when called in by my advisor. Finally, I asked my roommate to show me how she was studying this course, and with several all-day study sessions, I managed to pass. What a relief, because at that time if you failed a course, you could not continue in the program, and I wasn't used to failing in school."

Gloria recalls that zoology was tough, but she enjoyed the lab. "Once when we were dissecting a frog, Gwen's jumped off the table. We all screamed, but she picked it up and we continued on with the carving."

Their three nursing classes presented an overview of nursing, covering its history, various fields, and opportunities within the profession. These classes offered a place for them to interface with the nursing faculty.

"I had some exposure to the nursing profession because my mother, a nurse, and her friends who worked in various nursing areas had shared their experiences with me," Bette says. "In these classes I felt like a real nursing student, even though we didn't step inside a hospital this first year. It felt great to be at UNC, learning from the best."

The nursing courses were held in the sociology building, which was close to the Smith Dorm. "I liked the location but felt removed from being in nursing because there was no hospital, no uniforms, and no patients," Winnie says. "We only talked about nursing."

For Sally, learning about the areas in which a nurse might work led her to decide on public health nursing. "The idea of helping people be healthy appealed to me," she says. "I liked the teacher, Ms. Boyles, and enjoyed talking to her about what I was learning and how exciting it all was. I feared that my classmates thought I was brown-nosing, but I was more used to discussing my thoughts with adults than with my peers. I made the dean's list that first quarter. I was pleased but had already learned not to talk about that to my classmates either."

Gwen enjoyed the connections to the nursing faculty and Dean Kemble that the nursing classes brought. "Dean Kemble was so special. She was very professional and yet very personable. We knew when she meant business, and we all did our best to please her."

Sally placed out of English 101, and thus took religion as her first elective. "For the first time in my life, I was exposed to biblical criticism. My religious upbringing had been rather fundamentalist. I had not met adults who questioned, as I always had, that God had directly dictated the Bible. The accepted view had been that any contradictions were the result of the reader's inability to understand. Much Bible reading had led me to the conclusion that this explanation was illogical. I found new meaning in the familiar words. The Bible was more meaningful rather than less so. Of course, I did not share this part of what I learned at home. The wicked university was already seen as a potentially corrupting influence."

"Anthropology opened a wider view of mankind and its origin, societies, and cultures," recalls Bette. "It helped prepare me for a future clinical nursing assignment, where I cared for a hospitalized Gypsy patient, the 'Queen Mother.' During this experience all her family camped out in her hospital room, and the entire staff adapted to meet the unique needs of their culture."

Sally remembers the anthropology teacher livening up the class by climbing up on the back of a chair to illustrate how a gibbon sat on a limb. Rae recalls that she had to look up the word anthropology, as it was a totally new word for her. "The professor wrote that I was 'prodigious,' and I had to look that up too," she says.

Winnie developed an ear infection and stayed in the infirmary during exam week of winter quarter. She had to stay over to make up the exams while everyone else went home.

After Christmas vacation, Bette was happy and grateful to begin second quarter. Both winter and spring quarters included lab hours for chemistry and zoology, which meant they had more hours of class than the average freshman. "I had a sense of accomplishment and knew I could make it from now on," she says. "I found a study buddy in Janet. Together we marched to Wilson Library every evening and plowed through the chemistry book, along with our other textbooks. It was a wonderful feeling to discover that I could actually understand what was being taught and keep up with the subject during the next two quarters."

Campus Activities

The integration of the nursing students into the greater university included clubs, various organizations, churches, class offices, sports, publications, honorary societies, and sororities. As residents of Smith Dorm, they were eligible to participate in extracurricular activities representing women's dorms.

"Joining the Splash Club was a must for me, as swimming was my passion," Bette says. "It provided an opportunity for skilled swimmers to participate in water ballet, rhythmic swimming demonstrations (today called synchronized swimming), and other events. The main event was the annual Water Show in the spring. I was accepted as a member and actively participated for the next four years, becoming its vice president my senior year. By then we had ten other nursing students in the Splash Club."

That fall all the coeds living in Smith Dorm chose Geri to represent the Smith Dorm in the yearbook's *Yackety Yack* Beauty Contest. "As fate would have it, the contest was scheduled for the same evening as our midterm chemistry exam (the bane of my existence)," says Geri. "I was in a fog the entire day. After the evening exam, I flew back to Smith Dorm, threw on my evening gown, and ran across Cameron Avenue to Memorial Hall. The judges chose me to be one of the women in the court of the Beauty Queen. To this day it only seems real because of the picture on page 345 of the 1952 *Yackety Yack*."

Many of the student nurses participated in the YWCA and played intramural sports. Donna says, "Bette, Arlene, and I liked basketball, maybe because we were all tall. The Splash Club was also a favorite of mine, but my winning sport was tetherball. Until then I never really appreciated being tall with a swift, left-handed swing. Other than winning a freckle contest, tetherball was my one and only championship. I will add that this was a consolation to my being cut during cheerleading tryouts when very cute and darling girls jumping around with pom-poms made the squad."

A romantic interest motivated Sally to try new campus activities. "I wanted Bob to ask me for a real date, but since he didn't, I participated in the campus organizations in which he was active. I joined the Carolina Political Union and the Baptist Student Union and also presented meditations to interested students and faculty each day at noon. These activities broadened my horizons. At the Carolina Political Union, I met politicians who came to campus for presentations—including Hubert Humphrey. How impressed I was to talk with a US senator. We also discussed political issues in weekly meetings. This was familiar territory for me, since political discussions at home are among my earliest memories."

Sally belonged to the United Student Fellowship at the Congregational Church. This group met only once a month, so she went to the Baptist Student Union the other three Sundays. "These organizations were not greatly different," Sally says. "But one of my friends, a daughter of a Baptist minister, would not attend the Baptist Student Union because it was 'too liberal.' That was my first introduction to the idea that there were such differences within that denomination. I had assumed all Baptist churches held about the same positions."

"The first twenty-seven of us were quite active in campus life," says Geri. "Some of us participated in intramural sports and won trophies, some participated in student offices and campus activities, and all of us had study time at the historic Wilson Library. A very new experience was visiting a fraternity house for dinner."

Janet recalls that Pat's sister, Ginger, was a member of a sorority and invited them to have dinner with her on several occasions. "I always enjoyed it, along with the exposure to sorority life," Janet says. "As an only child, it was very interesting to have 'sisters,' as they were called. Perhaps I would have pursued that avenue if we had not had our own sorority—our group of nurses."

One of the first suggestions of the faculty was to elect a temporary chairman of the School of Nursing class to coordinate class decisions and activities, and Janet was elected to this position. They later elected School of Nursing class officers, selecting Janet as president, Louise as vice president, Rae as secretary, Mary as treasurer, and Geri as class historian. Donna was elected to UNC's Student Party and to the UNC Freshman Class Officers for 1952 as social chairman.

*The nursing students tour the building that would
become the nurses' dorm when complete.*

During the fall of 1951, the hospital was almost complete, but the nursing dorm was in its early stages. "We would periodically go with a faculty member to view the site, see the progress, and imagine how it would look when finished," says Janet. "It was encouraging that the nurses would eventually have a home."

As the first class, the freshman student nurses had the daunting task of designing their uniform, cap, and pin. "After many meetings at night to brainstorm and share ideas, we finally

*The UNC Chapel Hill
School of Nursing pin.*

decided on a navy-blue dress with white trim and white apron," Janet recalls. "Many designs for the cap were reviewed, as it could not duplicate any other in existence." The cap would distinctly identify the school, and the one they designed was most impressive with UNC embroidered on the left side. "We were all proud to wear it when we began patient care during our sophomore year and in all the years to follow," Janet says.

The school pin, not needed before the first class graduated in 1955, took longer to design. Sally chaired the pin committee, composed of faculty members and students from other classes who researched and designed various versions over several years. The committee's final design, contributed by Barbara Hedberg Self, class of 1957, was selected for the School of Nursing pin.

Dean Kemble

The foundation and underlying strength in pioneering the University of North Carolina School of Nursing was undisputedly due to its founding dean, Elizabeth Kemble. Her breadth of view, insight, wisdom, and innate ability to effectively persuade and champion her vision were truly pivotal for the state of North Carolina and for the University of North Carolina. "Dean Kemble was stately, personable, and spoke authoritatively with precise diction. When she was really smiling about something, she had dimples," Donna recalls.

Janet recalls how important faculty members were, especially Dean Kemble. "On one occasion, she invited us to her home for a cookout and a relaxing evening together. This was a side of her we rarely had the privilege of seeing: casually dressed in her slacks and sweater, in a lounge chair, happily smiling with twinkling eyes as we exchanged impromptu dialogue concerning current issues, whether academic or social. She listened intently and related on a personal level. This was such a pleasant memory for us."

During their visit, they met Dean Kemble's housemate, who spoke of enjoying their quiet home with the surrounding acreage of trees and land that allowed ample space for a garden and small chicken farm. What a great change and relief from the professional challenges faced daily at the School of Nursing by Dean Kemble.

The picnic and chickens inspired Donna to fulfill her speech assignment the next day by presenting Dean Kemble to her public speaking class. "I titled it 'Of Chickens and Deans,' a takeoff from 'Of cabbages and kings,' one of the quotes in Lewis Carroll's 'The Walrus and the Carpenter.' It seemed inspired to me at the time because Dean Kemble was pointedly goal oriented; she also took care of the 'nitty-gritty' of the program."

The dean had to make many decisions about her girls, some more unusual than others. Over the years, Janet had appeared in several school and community benefit programs as a tap dancer. "When the time came for the Miss Chapel Hill pageant, several town merchants approached me regarding the opportunity to represent them," Janet says. "They had remembered me because the talent portion was a major consideration. There was a bit of hesitation on my part. Our schedule was so busy, and the entire process had to be approved by Dean Kemble. I did meet with her and was not surprised that she did not approve, as it was 'not quite the image we should portray.' So, I graciously declined the offers, and my alternate career choice—to become a New York Radio City Rockette—ended quite abruptly."

Summer Vacation

The summer of 1952 provided a much needed vacation of three months, the longest break the nursing students would get during their four years. Summer-school classes and clinical assignments during their second and third years left them only four weeks of summer vacation.

Joy remembers realizing toward the end of the year that she wasn't going to make it. "Organic chemistry had taken its toll. I called my daddy at his second business in Raleigh, and asked (begged) him to take me home the next time he went to Charlotte. I knew Daddy was going to be furious with me. Instead, he was kind, thoughtful, and loving. He stated that he understood there were several openings in Charlotte for clerks at Roses, Woolworth's, and McLellan Dime Stores. Suffice it to say, I turned his offer down, took a summer-school class at Queens College in Charlotte, and passed organic chemistry with a flying C plus."

During the summer, Janet was a waitress at her parents' restaurant, The Pines. She often worked there while not in school, and many UNC summer-school students also frequented the restaurant. "I noticed a young man who visited often, and how he always managed to be seated at one of my assigned tables," she says. "I was cordial to all customers but was never allowed to linger at a table of boys. My conversations with this particular gentleman were kept to a minimum, as he often dined with friends. He was always friendly, had a pleasant demeanor, and was smartly dressed. He was quite dapper in his blue suede shoes.

"One day, a high school classmate dropped by the restaurant and told me that she knew a boy who was 'dying to date me,' but he wanted her to set up the date as we did not know each other. Initially, I was hesitant because I was not fond of blind dates, but I reluctantly agreed," Janet says. That evening, Janet's date, Bill Littlejohn, called, and they decided to leave from the restaurant the next day after her shift was over at 8:00 p.m.

"I changed clothes and was busily finishing up last-minute tasks at work in anticipation of my soon-to-arrive blind date. Who should walk into the restaurant but the cute boy I had noticed all summer. I thought to myself, 'Darn, here *he* is, and I have to leave with some blind date.' With my mind racing, I mustered up a smile and managed to get out a few words: 'You're traveling a little late tonight—where are all your buddies?' He quickly replied, 'No, I didn't come to eat, I came to pick you up for our date—I'm Bill Littlejohn.' What a wonderful surprise. We laughed, made quick introductions to my mom and dad (although my mom knew I had my eye on him for quite some time), and quickly left on our date. We had known each other all along—and those blue suede shoes looked especially nice that night. We saw the movie *High Noon*, drank hot chocolate at the drive-in, and I was home by curfew."

Many dates followed this great evening. After Janet and Bill became engaged, he shared his comments after that first date. When he returned to his dorm, his roommate asked how he liked his date, to which he quickly replied, "I would marry her tomorrow without a question." Bette and Arlene, who were also from Morganton, were especially happy for Janet and Bill, because they were instrumental in encouraging the relationship.

Bette began her vacation by traveling on a bus with her sister across the country to join their mom and dad in California. "Each round-trip bus ticket cost fifty dollars, all our family could afford after paying for two students to attend college for the past nine months," Bette says. "Dad had recently retired from the army, after two years in Japan during the Korean War. He now worked as a civilian at Camp Roberts in California, and it was my first time there. What fun it was to visit Hollywood and places heard about but not seen until then."

---

[3] See a full copy of the rules online at http://dc.lib.unc.edu/cdm/search/collection/nchh/searchterm/NCHH-123/order/identi.

3

Sophomore Year

The newly completed nurses' dorm.

One year after twenty-seven nursing students entered UNC's new School of Nursing, seventeen of them returned as sophomores in the fall of 1952. They were eager to start another year of course work and begin clinical nursing practice.

Janet's sophomore year began early because she was an orientation counselor for the new freshmen. "As a counselor, I was responsible for familiarizing five nursing students with the campus, including places to eat and socialize, as well as providing answers to their questions. It was a gratifying role to know we had new students to follow us on the page we began."

The rest of the nursing students returned to Chapel Hill in September and temporarily checked into the fourth floor of the new North Carolina Memorial Hospital because the School of Nursing building and the nurses' dormitory were not yet complete. The hospital had just admitted its first patients on September 2, but they stayed on other floors. The sophomore and freshman (class of 1956) nursing students slept in hospital beds and used the patients' tall and narrow metal cabinets to hang their clothes and a few drawers to hold their belongings.

The fourth floor also housed the hospital morgue, and on many occasions the girls were awakened by the sound of gurneys being wheeled past their doorways. "It was a scary feeling to hear this during the very last hour of the day," says Joy. "The sound of the gurneys crept in with the nighttime sounds of good night echoing in the halls. The ghostly feelings were never ending."

Janet remembers that the empty gurneys were a source of fun for some of the more mischievous girls. "I don't think our instructors were aware that a few students rode the gurneys to see how fast they would go and maybe had a race or two," she says.

If the nursing students had a visitor, the hospital information desk in the lobby phoned their floor. The girls rode elevators to leave their home floor, sometimes with books in hand and other times in evening dresses to meet dates for special occasions. They often joined hospital personnel, patients, and family members in the elevator.

"One evening, I was dressed for the fall German Club dance in a red satin and net, strapless gown," Janet recalls. "As I rode down the elevator to meet my date, a patient's family was also on the same elevator. I do not know what they thought of the 'lady in red' as they stared at me at the entire time. I kept my eyes glued to the elevator door hoping it would soon open."

Martha remembers the absence of locks on their doors. "The only security was maybe a night watchman for the entire complex. The elevators opened directly into the hall of our rooms, and my room was the closest to the elevators, which seemed to have a mind of their own. They opened throughout the night with an audible whoosh."

One time a group of the nursing students took a break on the rock wall in front of the new hospital. Five or six of them were eating a snack, laughing, talking, waving at other students, and saying hello to people coming and going from the hospital. "Suddenly a car stopped in front of us, and who should get out but Dean Kemble," recalls Janet. "Needless to say, she was not happy. In her deep voice, which we recognized all too well, she quite sternly declared, 'Girls! This is *not* an appropriate place for nurses to sit. You appear to be in another profession.' We promptly dispersed, avoided all rock walls thereafter, and chose other places to congregate."

Moving into the Off-Campus Nurses' Dorm

The experience of living in the hospital was exciting, but the nursing students joyfully moved into their very own nurses' dorm on November 18. Since faculty members had taken turns spending the night with the students in the hospital, they too were glad that the new dorm was finished.

The new nurses' dorm included a library.

The nurses' dorm had new furniture, selected with the help of faculty member Mrs. Alice Gifford. "We had our own library and parlors with TVs (a new thing on the market)," recalls Winnie. "The recreation room had a Ping-Pong table and a piano and was large enough for parties. We had a wonderful housemother, Mrs. Roberta Brower, who enforced rules for closed study, curfews, hours for telephone calls, and expected behavior. In hindsight, I'm sure this helped us mature and accomplish our purpose for being there." Mary recalls that their dates could come to the lobby and request the person on duty to call the students in their rooms to come down and meet their dates.

Janet was now rooming with Winnie. "I found her to be congenial, thoughtful, neat, organized, and always there to share my joys and concerns. She was dedicated and blessed with good nursing skills, and I knew she had found the perfect profession. What a wonderful friend then, and through the years."

Donna roomed with Sara, and she grew used to their dark-green chenille bedspreads that attracted smoke like a magnet. "Late at night we'd listen to WRR's Our Best to You. The boys at State, Duke, and UNC would call in to dedicate a song to their girlfriends, and it would be announced if she were at Duke, UNC, Peace, Meredith, St. Mary's, or even a certain high school. Sara and I never did hear our names mentioned with someone dedicating a song to us like 'Smoke Gets in Your Eyes' or 'Unforgettable.'

"Sara was constant," Donna recalls. "She could be serious, and she was certainly fun. One evening I came in and she had stuffed a full-length mattress in my closet, so when I opened the door to step in, my nose was touching the black-and-white-striped ticking. I was speechless, and she was laughing heartily, eyes flashing. For the next hour, she had a giggly snicker and laughing eyes as I tried to get the mattress out of the closet, and we both knew she had carried out the best prank of the year."

Some of the students took a beach trip to Fort Macon, North Carolina. Pictured are Gloria, Virginia, and Winnie (bottom) with Louise and Gwen (middle).

Not long after moving into the nurses' dormitory, Geri was asked to visit Dean Kemble in her office. "I couldn't imagine what I had done to merit this. I learned from our dean that she had received a letter from my mother expressing her concern that I had 'lost my religion' at Carolina. I tried but could not think of anything to explain Mom's distress. During a later visit home, I found a letter that Dean Kemble had written to my mom after she talked with me. She wrote that we had talked, and that I was an intelligent and levelheaded young woman who was doing well at Carolina. Any changes in my attitude were probably as a result of experiencing so many new ideas in that first year away from home. She would always be available for parents and/ or her students no matter what they wanted to discuss with her."

The nurses' dormitory sat between the dormitory for the North Carolina Memorial Hospital's intern and resident staff and the School of Nursing building, which connected to the four-hundred-bed main hospital and other health-affairs schools. These buildings were about half a mile off the university's main campus—a good walk to and from campus courses. However, for nursing courses and clinical assignments, it was a matter of steps from the dorm to the classrooms in the School of Nursing as well as to the hospital.

There Go the Nurses

That fall, campus classes included general psychology and introductory physics. These met daily Monday through Friday, and had lab hours in addition to class time. The basic nursing class was taught in the School of Nursing and at the hospital. So, back and forth they trekked.

Like many of them, Winnie remembers hustling to be on time for campus classes. "Many times you would hear the comment, 'There go the nurses. You can tell them by the way they walk.' If we had hospital hours that morning, we would run through the dorm, throw off our aprons and caps, grab our books, take the shortcut behind the zoology building (at the intersection of Pittsboro and Raleigh Roads), and race to class."

They entered their sophomore year with more confidence after all they had learned as freshmen. "We were now identified as 'nurses' since we were seen briskly walking everywhere on campus in our navy-blue dresses," Janet says. "It was a long hike from the hospital to campus with a mere ten minutes between classes. Somehow, we did it, and no one was overweight as a result."

"These walks kept us connected to our goals of a college education and becoming nurses," Bette says. "Being a nursing student brought rewards such as being noticed and admired. This year, the physics class was just for us, and it felt good to learn the basic fundamentals of physics. Our teacher skillfully gave lectures that included components related to patient care, such as the science behind X-rays or radiation treatments and the role of gravity in draining fluids or administering solutions. I also think we made the general psychology class and lab work more interesting for the instructor by being a change from teaching mostly boys."

The School of Nursing was an extension of the hospital, not a separate building. It contained two to three classrooms, a kitchen lab for nutrition classes, offices for the dean and faculty, a lounge area for faculty and staff, and a large auditorium shared with departments in the hospital.

"We thought it absolutely wonderful to be here in our own place," Bette remembers. They had beds, mannequin patients, an anatomical skeleton, and various instruments for taking vital signs. "Some evenings we would slip into the rooms and practice with the equipment."

However, Dean Kemble was not happy with the building and its location because it was not a single entity in itself with a proper main entrance, worthy of a professional school. It took time, the growth of the school, many struggles, and almost twenty years before the school would move into a new building.

New Uniforms and New Skills

At last the nursing students were introduced to basic nursing arts in their School of Nursing building and in a real hospital. "We learned to make a 'tight' bed, bathe patients, take a patient's temperature, pulse, and respiration (TPR), and take blood pressure as well as how to tidy the bedside unit, relate to patients, read charts, and record observations on the nurses' notes portion of the chart," Bette says.

Winnie recalls that being in the hospital and eating in its cafeteria with the "real medical people" made them realize that they were on their way. "I remember that learning was exciting, and I wanted to know more," she says. "This was certainly reinforced by our hospital hours."

The instructors stressed the importance of explaining to patients what would be done in any procedure to help anticipate their questions and ease apprehension. The explanation was especially important for complex procedures, such as catheterizations, where sterile technique was essential.

The nursing students wore their uniforms for the first time during their sophomore year. First row: Winnie, Sally, Joy, Janet, Donna, Virginia. Second row: Pat, Rae, Mary, Sara, Geri, Bette, Arlene, Gloria, Gwen, Martha, Louise.

They were taught to observe patients for physical and mental abnormalities and to be good listeners. "This was an invaluable lesson, as a nurse often hears more in their daily care than the doctor," Janet says. "We recorded symptoms in the patient's chart, and at report time the head nurse gave the information to the next shift of nurses for continuity of care. Physicians also read the nurse observations to assist in further evaluation of patient care. As the year progressed, we became involved in more treatments, procedures, and skills integral to patient care."

For the first time they wore the uniforms and nursing caps they had designed. There was no nursing cap ceremony, typical of other schools of nursing. "I was proud to wear the navy-blue dress with a white collar and white cuffs around the short sleeves when attending classes," Bette says. "We added the wraparound, white, starched bib apron and nursing cap when in the hospital with patients."

The first time Bette wore her full uniform in the hospital, she could not help admiring herself in the mirror while she emptied a washbasin in a patient's bathroom. "I must have taken longer than expected, because my instructor, Ms. Ruth Dalrymple, came to check on me and caught me looking at myself. She never said a word, apparently understanding my embarrassment."

Donna was wearing her cap with the embroidered *UNC*, when she walked into a semiprivate room to care for a new patient. "One of the men started grinning at me, and the first thing he said was, 'Oh, I see you're in the United Nurses Corps.'"

The nursing students also enjoyed dressing up for special occasions. That winter Gloria and Virginia attended a dance that the Winston Dorm gave for the nursing students. "I met Don at this event, and we danced the evening away. I was quite impressed that he brought me back to the nurses' dorm in a cab," Gloria says. "My social life improved after meeting Don. We attended big dances, called Germans. We also attended a Memorial Hall concert that included big bandleaders Ray

Anthony, Tommy and Jimmy Dorsey, and Louis Armstrong. That was a fun night."

The new freshman nursing class included a student from New Bern who played in the UNC band. "She asked a couple of us to go with two male friends to a banquet put on by the music fraternity," Winnie says. "My date turned out to be my husband of forty-seven years, and the two of us later settled in New Bern."

Winnie remembers venturing to Sara's camp in Marshallberg, North Carolina. "Virginia obtained her parents' car from Durham, and she, Sara, Lou, Gloria, Gwen, and I drove to Marshallberg. We had a wonderful time wading in the sound, boat riding, and having an oyster/clam roast that evening. We had such a good time that we were late leaving. Realizing that we could not make Chapel Hill before the dorm was closed, we crashed at Sara's parents' house in New Bern and left in the wee hours. We arrived at the hospital at 6:00 a.m., just in time to shower, eat, and make 8:00 a.m. class. The class happened to be demonstrating bed baths in one of the hospital units. Unfortunately, I was chosen to be the patient, and what a time I had trying to stay awake. I certainly received a few looks from my instructor."

Bill and Janet dated steadily this year. "Our love for one another grew, so the decision was made for marriage at this time rather than after graduation," says Janet. "Our parents gave us their blessing, but a larger hurdle was to meet with Dean Kemble to receive her permission to remain in school while married. Married students were new to nursing schools, and I was not sure she approved of this change. This was a major challenge for us to meet with her—a stressful event. Many questions and platitudes

Janet and Bill, 1952.

finally led to her approval. She advised us to work together and support the commitment to our goals we had set for ourselves—and above all, to be happy. A final smile from Dean Kemble and a sigh of relief from us completed the scenario as the door closed behind us. Our wedding ceremony was held on August 2, 1953.”

Early Hospital Experiences

Polio cases on campus brought about the cancelation of two home football games that fall.[4] As the nursing students began clinical experiences, they saw the polio epidemic firsthand. Winnie remembers being awed at seeing polio patients in iron lung machines in the hospital.

“Many of my early nursing experiences were in the hospital’s 3 West unit, which cared for colored patients,” Bette says. “The terms black and African American were not used then, and segregation was tolerated throughout the South. The head nurse for 3 West, Dorothy Aeschliman, RN, knew how to meet the needs of her patients while also mentoring the unit staff and nursing students. She helped introduce the nursing student as a new role that was under the authority of the School of Nursing and independent of the hospital and its staff.”

Four students and one instructor made a clinical group, and each group was assigned to a different patient unit. “My congenial group included Arlene, Gloria, and Gwen, and we stayed together for clinical rotations throughout our sophomore year,” Bette says. They received minimum wage, seventy-five cents an hour, for work in the clinical areas. They worked enough to make about twelve dollars every week, which came in handy for buying meals.

Geri remembers being surprised that she was expected to hand a urinal to male patients and empty the results. “I had assumed that would be the job of male orderlies, but I soon got over it,” she says. “My most upsetting experience was in the emergency room. I was assisting a doctor with a procedure, when I got confused about what I was to do next. The doctor blurted out, 'Do you work here or are you just a decoration?' Totally mortified, I burst into tears and ran and hid in the ladies' room. I can't recall the outcome, but to this day I avoid the ladies' room in any emergency room."

One of Martha's patients was the son of a UNC administrator. "For several weeks, he came to the hospital, ate breakfast with the nursing students, and then went to see his son and help with his morning care. One morning, we were all at breakfast as usual. When I arrived at the patient's room, I was told that the son had died during the night. He had returned to have breakfast and silently say good-bye to us student nurses."

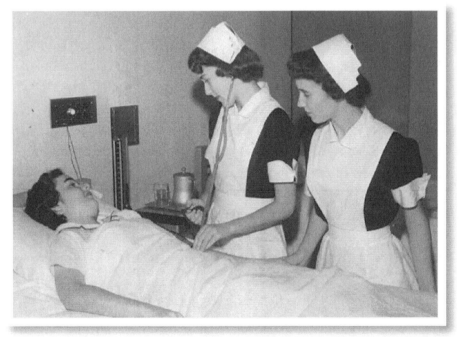

Rae and Janet practice taking the blood pressure of their classmate Louise.

School of Nursing instructors made the clinical assignments, and they emphasized learning experiences rather than serving the hospital. This approach was different from the way other nursing students received training in North Carolina at that time, and it aroused some resistance from staff nurses and physicians, who said the students wouldn't have enough clinical hours to work as real nurses when they graduated.

"Having an instructor supporting us gave me confidence and helped me believe in this new approach for nursing education," Bette says. "Together, we were creating something different and important."

Their knowledge and communication skills were expanding, and sometimes learning took place when least expected. "During an early clinical experience in the hospital, I was assigned to a patient who was nauseated," Bette remembers. "I held a basin while he vomited into it. Before I knew it, we were both heaving into that basin. In walks my instructor, Ms. Findlay. I said, 'I am so sorry I threw up.' She replied, 'Ms. Davis, everything will be all right, but please remember to use the word *regurgitate*.' She asked another classmate, Rae, who was working in another room, to go with me to the dorm. It wasn't until our fiftieth reunion that Rae mentioned how it had affected her. While we walked back, I held onto my folded, smelly apron, as I had missed most of the basin. Rae helped me get settled and then made it to her own room just in time before repeating my earlier incident of regurgitating."

Making Their Mark

Participating in professional activities at the state level expanded the students' knowledge of nursing leaders and history, and broadened their view of the health-care field of which they were now members. Joy and freshman Elaine Allison served tea at the governor's mansion on November 6 in celebration of the North Carolina State Nurses' Association's Golden Anniversary. Other student nurses from throughout the state participated.

Janet was elected as secretary of the state North Carolina Student Nurses' Association. "I presented the minutes of the previous year at the annual meeting of the association," Janet says. "I was somewhat apprehensive, as this was the largest group I had ever addressed. As an officer, I was chosen along with Sara, as historian, to represent North Carolina at the National Student Nurses Convention that summer in Cleveland, Ohio. It was a wonderful experience to represent our new school and to share all our 'firsts' with other established, well-known nursing programs from across the country. It was evident just how far we had come in our methodology with determination and dedication, as we received many accolades for our progress in nursing education."

That spring, the University of North Carolina dedicated the North Carolina Memorial Hospital together with the School of Nursing, School of Medicine, and School of Dentistry. Dean Kemble had managed to keep the school on equal ground with the other health-affairs schools.

Courses during the winter and spring quarters on campus included sociology, political science, and foods and nutrition as well as bacteriology with lab. There were also advanced nursing courses with clinical assignments in the School of Nursing or the hospital. Still on the quarter system, all the classes met Monday through Friday, usually with homework every day for each course. The nursing students often wondered who would be the next to leave.

"It was exhausting at times," Bette says. "So much so that when we were learning basic principles of medicine and about medical conditions, Sara and I thought we must have a thyroid problem and made a visit to the student infirmary. The physician assured us we were okay and that it was common for new students in medicine or nursing to experience the condition being studied. Nevertheless, he said to have blood tests taken, and he would inform us of the results. After that meeting, we decided not to have the blood tests. However, in a few days, Sara received a phone call from his office saying our thyroid tests were normal."

"Every day was a new experience," Gwen says. "Some days were overwhelming. Classes were very difficult, especially political science and foods and nutrition. But it is the friendships we developed, always helping one another, along with the beautiful campus of Chapel Hill, that remain in my mind."

They were in the throes of "sophomoritis" during this time. "We gathered in the kitchen at the end of the dorm hall to vent, some questioning the idea of being a nurse," Bette says. "Fortunately, this period passed, and I now know this is typical for college sophomores."

Gwen remembers being called to her instructor's office. "It was suggested that I change my major and leave nursing. 'I'll show her,' was probably what she wanted me to think. I was determined to succeed and began to apply myself even more. I had not been studying as much because of a busy social life."

Sally knitted her way through bacteriology. "I learned that doing something with my hands kept my mind engaged with the subject matter better than writing copious notes that I would not use. Now I recorded only the most important facts. I could see how all this information would be useful as I moved into actually being a nurse. Up until now I had been learning only because the material was interesting at the moment, with no great intent at retention beyond the final exam."

Faculty from the Schools of Nursing and Medicine taught the nursing students Basic Principles of Nursing as well as Medicine Fundamental to Nursing Care. Aspects of anatomy, physiology, and pharmacology relating to a specific condition were integrated into the nursing courses. Concurrently, nursing instructors selected patients in the clinical areas that represented the conditions they studied in the classroom. The combination of classwork and patient load was very heavy, particularly if a patient required a lot of time and care.

"One of my patient's daughters must have noticed how hard I was working, as she gave me a copy of a poem the patient had written," Bette says. "The first few lines are: 'Tis not for less of work I ask, but more of strength, that I may do a larger task, and go full length, for work well done is heaven begun.'"

Summer Session

Mrs. Eloise Lewis arrived in June of 1953, in time to teach the surgical nursing courses. Gloria says that Mrs. Lewis was her most memorable nursing instructor. "She was so dynamic, a great leader and a great listener. She expected our best, and this encouraged us to do our best. She was always dressed very neatly." Bette describes Mrs. Lewis as a knowledgeable, hardworking, and exacting teacher in the hospital and classroom.

Bette was assigned to surgical patients with an orthopedic, urological, or gynecologic problem, each one bringing a new challenge in patient care. Caring for them required some necessary, but unpleasant, duties.

One of Bette's patients was a young African American teenage girl from a rural area who was transferred to North Carolina Memorial Hospital, which provided care for people from all over the state. She was in an isolation room because of her severe typhoid fever. Typhoid cases were rare even then and are quite rare today thanks to public health policies.

"Her poor body was wracked with pain because of intestinal hemorrhaging," Bette says. "She could not change positions unless helped, and it was important that I recorded all her fluid intake and output when changing her urinary bags, assisting with her multiple bowel movements or checking intravenous fluids. She needed rest and someone to be with her. She remained sick a long time, but did recover and go home."

Bette also learned a great deal when she cared for a young paraplegic patient, who was transferred from another facility because of an advanced sacral decubitus ulcer, also known as a bedsore. She recalls that he was put on a Stryker frame, which allowed staff to turn a patient's whole body easily and more frequently. The Stryker frame kept pressure off the patient's back and was rotated for feeding, care of the dorsal wound, and cleaning and applying soaks, etc. The technologically advanced Stryker frame is still in use today for care of patients with back or neck injuries and surgeries.

A small and important change was taking place in the sterilization of medical supplies, but it seemed uneventful then. The student nurses learned to give injections with glass syringes from a tray that was packaged, dated, and sterilized in a central sterilization area rather than at the unit level. The new method was more economically efficient and made better use of nursing staff. Other items used in sterile procedures, such as a bladder catheterization or a dressing change, were packaged, dated, sterilized, and kept in a central supply room until needed in a unit. "As antiquated as this method is today, it was a new time saver for hospitals," Bette says.

Six weeks in the operating room reinforced the importance of using sterile technique. During this rotation, they were assigned to either act as a scrub nurse, who wore a sterile gown, mask, and gloves while assisting the physicians at the operating table, or as a circulating nurse, who moved around the area attending to nonsterile items and any additional equipment.

"My first assignment was as a circulating nurse," Bette recalls. "I was crouched on the floor by the operating table, enthusiastically scooping up the dirty sponges that had missed the gauze bucket. I saw one coming toward the bucket and grabbed it out of a gloved hand about to drop it. I heard a voice say, 'Change my glove, she touched it.' At the other end of the hand was the chief of surgery, Dr. Warner Wells. I wanted to disappear into the floor. Nevertheless, I gained awareness of what patients undergo during surgery and of operating-room teamwork."

Winnie remembers that one morning during her orthopedics rotation she heard a female patient moaning and hollering, almost continuously. "Somehow I knew Mrs. Lewis was going to assign me that patient for the week," she says. "I went in with fear and trepidation, but the patient and I survived, and there was indeed a sense of accomplishment in making the patient more comfortable."

Winnie also recalls the time that an orthopedic surgeon lined up a group of students and their instructor and told them to go into a room, look at the wound, not react, and return to the hall. "A cast had been cut open, and we could see an open ulcerated area at the wrist near the radial nerve. The surgeon then began to lecture us, saying, 'I suppose this was reported.' I had taken care of the patient the previous week, and promptly said, 'Yes, sir, it was.' I didn't look at Mrs. Lewis for fear of her reaction."

The injury to the wrist indicated an improperly applied cast and lack of proper response and attention by the nurses to the swelling, temperature, discoloration, and pulse changes that would indicate a problem. Winnie explains that she was concerned that as a student she had had the audacity to speak back to the doctor. The students were taught to respect the physicians as the authority figures in patient care. For example, they would move from the chart desk or seats at the desk when doctors came to make rounds. "I fully expected to be chastised or graded down by my instructor, but there were no repercussions to the incident, thank goodness, and the surgeon just nodded his head at my response."

Mary remembers summer school as more relaxed but still demanding. "On the main campus, a Watermelon Festival was held, and I was thrilled to be an entry for queen," she says. "Summer also meant we could swim in the outdoor Olympic-size pool, and I did, every chance I could manage," Bette says. "There is nothing like floating on water, under the sun, and letting your mind drift."

---

[4] Home football games against North Carolina State and Georgia were canceled. Read more about how the campus responded to the polio outbreak: http://blogs.lib.unc.edu/uarms/index.php/2012/10/health-alert-polio-outbreak-on-unc-campus-unc-nc-state-football-game-cancelled/#sthash.4q6nGK3P.dpuf.

4

Junior Year

Bette (second from left), Mary, Sara, Donna, and Rae with sophomores, Ruth and Jane, who are in their uniforms.

When the nursing students returned to class in September of 1953, UNC had changed to a semester system with fall and spring semesters and a summer session. Classes met every other day Monday through Saturday, which gave them a little extra time to juggle homework and absorb content.

"I felt the difference right away and liked it," Bette recalls. "This schedule also meant that Christmas and spring breaks provided some down time before returning for final papers and exams at the end of each semester."

This year, the School of Nursing admitted its third class, the class of 1957. The school was growing, and the students filled the dorm. Bette was elected dorm president. "Seeing freshman faces excited about orientation and joining older students boosted my pride," she recalls.

Gwen enjoyed spending more time in the hospital working with patients. "The younger nursing students were often involved with our class, but we stayed with our class members the majority of the time," she recalls. "Dean Kemble remained a key person in our motivation to do the best we could. I had been separated from my twin sister, Gloria, since our sophomore year in labs and hospital assignments. The instructors kept getting us confused, and it became easier if we were in different locations. This was a big adjustment, as we had always been together. It was also good because we became more independent and grew closer to other classmates."

Gloria remembers that classes seemed easier, because either classes were not as challenging, or the nursing students had improved their study habits and were better at organizing their precious free time. "Don and I spent many a late evening at the main library on campus," Gloria says. "We would go to Lenoir Hall for apple pie and ice cream after studying. The pie and ice cream came to just a quarter."

Fall semester classes seemed natural to Bette. "Obstetric nursing, pediatric nursing, marriage, and child development were all interrelated and personally useful, and the teachers and instructors were enthusiastic and stimulating," she recalls. "Of all my nursing course books, the

OB-GYN book was the only one of which I read every word. Ms. Ruth Lindberg, so knowledgeable and grandmotherly, loved what she taught and made this class fascinating. I knew that if a mother was concerned about her baby being born prematurely, I could share with her that I was born prematurely and turned out healthy. Concurrently, we learned about child development. I enjoyed this class and easily remembered the material as we moved through a child's normal progressive stages."

The sociology course on marriage covered the family, society, and life events. The students were asked to write a paper exploring their self-views and growth in relation to the course's content. "I wrote about what truly mattered to me and how I was changing, which I think contributed to the A I received on the paper," Bette says. Winnie recalls being chagrined to later read her husband's essay assignment for this class and found out that he had a more grounded approach to marriage and family than she did.

Janet began her junior year as a newlywed. "We forgot most of the traditional habits of newlyweds because our educational responsibilities were more important and we could share them," she says. "After spring semester, Bill finished college and went into the air force. All men over eighteen were obliged to serve in the armed forces once they graduated. I continued with the nursing program as I had planned."

Gloria remembers working in the hospital in the mornings and going to class all afternoon. "Most of this time we ate lunches in the hospital because of time constraints, and it was cheaper than eating uptown. Don and I would splurge on Sunday by going to the Carolina Coffee Shop for veal cutlets."

This was a busy year, as the nursing students began rotating through medical and surgical specialties, including pediatrics, obstetrics, orthopedics, and the operating room. "At the end of each rotation, a case study was assigned that included the patient, disease, symptoms, prognosis, treatment, and nursing care," Janet says. "This paper, clinical performance, classroom exams, and final exams constituted our final grade."

Working with children on the pediatric unit proved to be both heartwarming and heartbreaking for Bette. She recalls that their earnest instructor, Ms. Beulah Gautefald, was a very patient, small woman who loved children. North Carolina Memorial Hospital received children from counties all over the state because of its expertise in diagnosis and treatment.

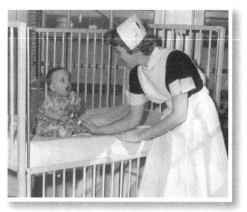

Geri cares for a pediatric patient at North Carolina Memorial Hospital.

These children were very sick, sometimes terminal. "One toddler's body and face were so edematous from chronic nephritis that she hurt all over, even when touched," Bette says.

"My case study was a young boy with leukemia," Janet says. "He was truly a delight to care for. I remember his bright eyes and smile, even now as I write." Winnie particularly enjoyed the pediatric unit and caring for a young man who had survived tetanus, the wound being barely discernible, she says.

Going to the playroom helped get little minds off casts, bandages, and IV poles and provided a place for the children to be with family members. "In my innocence, I commented to a mother of a child with Down syndrome about how the little girl was usually smiling or laughing," Bette recalls. "The mother explained that was characteristic of the syndrome."

As Christmas and cold weather approached, the nursing students saw more children with burns from falling against kerosene stoves, wood stoves, or open fireplaces. The burns covered most of the children's bodies, and for weeks they stayed alone in isolated rooms. Only while enduring the changing of soaked-gauze wrappings several times a day was a staff member or student with them. Most families did not live close enough to visit often. "I talked, sang songs, or told nursery stories when they were not screaming," Bette says. "Today burn treatment is quicker and more humane."

Janet found the obstetrics rotation the most gratifying. "There is no way to accurately describe—nor will I ever forget—the first delivery and the miracle of childbirth," she says. "I thoroughly enjoyed this clinical area, and I can now see why I spent many years in that field after graduation. My case study was a young mother with postpartum depression."

Joy remembers that one of her first surgical experiences as a nursing student was in the orthopedic surgical arena. "A physician debriding the big toe of an elderly male patient observed that the operative area was gangrenous and immediately amputated the digit," Joy says. "He then proceeded to throw the very useless digit to one of the circulating student nurses. I'll never tell who caught the toe with her bare hands. The next day, there was much screaming, yelling, and crying from the nursing students after they found out that the physician decided to amputate the left leg to which the toe had belonged. The doctors and nurses flew around getting ready for the event. The silvery saw was sharp, and the patient was prepped sitting up, staring straight ahead. The surgeon began carefully sawing at the knee, but even with the suction apparatus, the patient could still hear the awful saw-bone noise. Someone suggested that we sing as loud as we could. The patient requested 'Shall We Gather at the River,' and we were happy to oblige."

The operating room rotation was another favorite for Janet. "I remember the first major surgery I observed: the incision in the skin was made, the bleeding began, and then the instruments began moving so quickly, especially the hemostats to stop the bleeding so that the surgery could proceed. The concentration and skilled movements of the surgeon and nurse were impressive. Many firsts come to mind as I progressed: scrubbing and gowning to be the scrub nurse; exposure of the heart and observing this fascinating beating organ; holding the basin for an organ being removed; delicately threading a needle as quickly as possible; and the all-important sponge count. Each sponge was counted prior to surgery, and used sponges were placed on a sheet for counting before closure of the surgical site. The number had to match to be sure no sponges were left inside the patient. Handing the instruments to the surgeon correctly and as he preferred sometimes became a challenge, because each physician had his own particular routine, and some doctors were certainly more temperamental than others. It was important to be a good listener with an even better memory."

Spring Semester

Spring semester was a whole new ball game. It was hectic for the nursing students because their campus course schedule depended on their clinical rotation. Mary remembers having to sometimes remove her crisp white apron and wear the blue dress to classes when there was not enough time to change.

One rotation was spent at the Victory Village Children's Day Care Center, which opened in 1953 as a parent cooperative. It was located off of Manning Drive near the hospital, and close to the Victory Village neighborhood that housed the many married veterans and their families who were going to school on the GI bill after World War II.

"Our rotation into Victory Village Children's Day Care Center gave us opportunities to see another side of the student population at

UNC—students with families and normal, healthy, growing children," says Winnie.

"For my clinical group, our time at the Victory Village Children's Day Care Center was scheduled just before the on-campus American history class," Bette recalls. "With a greater distance to walk or run to campus, and because I usually couldn't leave the center on time (children can't be left on the potty, for example), I was chronically late for the class. I missed the first ten to fifteen minutes of each lecture. Added to that, I had my only cold in years, likely caught from the children since they all had colds and runny noses."

The American history textbook was massive, and the required reading for the American fiction course included novels such as Joseph Conrad's *Heart of Darkness* and Ernest Hemingway's *A Farewell to Arms*. "Sometimes, several of us were up all night in the kitchen reading and preparing for tests," Bette says.

"American history was a bear. The instructor gave essay tests all semester then gave blanks and multiple choice for the final, or else vice versa. Whichever, it was terrible," says Gloria.

Typically, when there is too much to do and not enough time, something has to give. "I ended American history with my second and last D," Bette says. "Virginia helped me write one paper, but I had not studied enough and got too far behind.

One of the professors Janet remembers the most is Dr. Bernard Boyd, who taught Religion 28, the Old Testament. "To acquire class attention, Dr. Boyd would relate a book in the Bible to a current situation everyone understood," she says. "I still recall his edification of the Book of Esther: The king was having a beauty contest, and after he saw Esther in her black bathing suit, he knew she had to be his wife. No one else had a chance. Dr. Boyd had everyone's full attention now, and the Bible was our new favorite book."

The nursing students won first prize for their skit in the Sigma Chi Derby.

Joy (far left) was a finalist in the "Miss Modern Venus" contest.

It wasn't all work for the student nurses. They were, and still are, a fun-loving group. When they get together, they reminisce about the fun times. One occasion that especially comes to mind occurred in the spring of 1954 during the sixth annual Sigma Chi Derby.

Every spring coed groups competed in amusing or conventional contests during the Sigma Chi Derby in Kenan Stadium. The School of Nursing's entry, "Hill Billies," consisted of singers and a stringed combo. "We played a big washtub with a broom for the string bass, strummed a washboard, played a real guitar, banged on pots, and took an occasional swig from an empty moonshine bottle," Bette recalls. "Our motif consisted of overalls, jeans, plaid shirts, straw hats, blackened teeth, and bare feet. At the end of our performance, the only thing heard was dead silence. I instantaneously took the microphone and said, 'We are hell when we're well, but we have been right sick lately,' trying to make some kind of an excuse. We got a roaring response from the crowd." The nurses had recovered, and their entry won first prize.

A highlight of the derby was the "Miss Modern Venus" contest, in which beautiful contestants in shorts and heels were judged as they walked past the stands of delighted spectators. Joy was one of the twelve selected finalists. Another event called "Strip to the Flesh" required coeds to remove their clothes down to a bathing suit. Bette was ahead of the pack until her hose got caught on her shoes.

"We certainly were maturing, and some of us were making major life decisions on mates and marriage," says Winnie. "The change of pace into the semester system did seem to give us more time, but any spare time was filled with boyfriends and campus activities: Sunday afternoon concerts on the lawn, winter concerts in Hill Hall, Playmaker's productions, and always the basketball and football games."

The boys in Aycock Dorm invited the student nurses to a cookout in October. "Bette suggested I attend, and it was there I met my future husband, Dean Butler from Morganton, who was also a twin," Gwen says. "He was a student in the pharmacy program. We spent a lot of time studying together in the main library and walked all over campus, giving us the exercise we needed."

Rae remembers that classmate Charles Kuralt wrote an article in the *Daily Tar Heel* in which he said he did not think of the nursing students as coeds. "At the dean's request I went to talk with him, but he was inflexible and would not print a retraction," recalls Rae. "There is, and never has been, in my mind, any doubt that we were coeds. I remember the dean and staff emphasizing, from the beginning, our school being a part of the whole university and encouraging us to participate in various campus activities."

Despite the criticism in the student newspaper, the nursing students were active on campus. Donna was a UNC class officer, serving as social chairman her freshman year, secretary as a junior, and treasurer as a senior. Gloria and Donna both worked on the *Yackety Yack* yearbook, too. In campus-wide elections for senior year, Geri ran for the office of secretary of student government and won the election. "It was amazing that one of our first twenty-seven freshmen in the School of Nursing was elected to such a major campus office," she says. "Largely because of my participation in campus student government, I was also inducted into The Order of the Old Well for our senior year."

Donna decided to go through rush and pledge Pi Beta Phi. "This added a distinctly new dimension to my last two years at UNC," she recalls. "It was like a second sorority, the first one being a nursing sorority, which was exclusive only to my nursing class. I was living in the nurses' dorm when the pledge bids arrived and had no idea that any of the campus girls even knew where the nursing students had moved after they left Smith Dorm, but I was happy they found my room."

During one summer session, Donna lived in the Pi Phi house and participated in university contests as a Pi Phi. "I also went to a football game in Washington, DC, with my sorority sisters," Donna says. "I truly enjoyed that association, and it expanded my view on many issues. In the final analysis, I identified more with my nursing peers because of the time and course intensity of the nursing program we shared. However, a distinct plus for joining a sorority was that when I moved to a new city or state, I had an immediate entree for meeting new friends and was readily associated with a group."

Gravely Sanatorium

Spring semester's nursing courses, taught by Mrs. Alice Gifford, included Principles of Public Health and Public Health Nursing, Communicable Diseases, and a clinical rotation of six weeks' experience in tuberculosis nursing in Gravely Sanatorium.

During the 1950s, tuberculosis was still prevalent. Gravely Sanatorium was considered state of the art when it opened in 1953, but that did not mean it was air-conditioned. However, the building had large windows that opened. Thankfully, with medication and better prevention, tuberculosis is no longer the threat it was.

Gravely was a tuberculosis sanatorium until 1975, when it became a center for treatment of cancer patients. In 2010, the building was replaced with a garden and labyrinth. "It was sad to see the old building torn down. I have driven many patients there to receive radiation for cancer," Gloria says.

During the time at Gravely Sanatorium, some of the nursing students thought they had symptoms of tuberculosis. Donna entered the rotation with some apprehension because of the infectiousness of tuberculosis and the Bacillus Calmette–Guérin (BCG) vaccine. "I harbored a nagging feeling that I didn't want to take the vaccine, but on the day it was given, I stuck out my arm with the same sinking sensation as when I once jumped off the highest diving board on a dare.

I adhered meticulously to the protective protocols of gowning and hand washing."

There was palpable enthusiasm for a new medication treatment at this time—a triple therapy, meaning it was three drugs given together. "As a student I felt exhilarated about being on the cutting edge of medicine," Donna says. "Over time, the medication therapy was successful and cure rates were established. Unfortunately, drug-resistant strains are still being aggressively treated today."

Winnie remembers that the rotation to Gravely Sanatorium helped lay to rest her many fears regarding tuberculosis and communicable diseases. "The rooms were very clean, patients and nurses strictly adhered to protocol, and the atmosphere was more relaxed than acute-care units. I think the patients enjoyed the student nurses, and some of them shared their talents with us. For example, I learned to crochet."

Janet says this rotation was an opportunity to learn isolation techniques. "Many patients were sent to our hospital from smaller hospitals that did not have the necessary equipment for appropriate patient care. This was certainly the case with tuberculosis."

One of Donna's patients at Gravely was a Chinese gentleman who spoke no English. "I was gowned with hands meticulously washed, while he walked around in his street clothes and did not appear to be sick at all," she says. "Since we could not converse with each other, we played Chinese checkers and smiled at each other when we had more than a couple of jumps. He would deliberately and discretely count his jumps in Chinese. I listened intently to the sound of each word, until one day I had five jumps. As I jumped each marble, I took a leap and said, 'Eeee, arrr, sahm, soo, wooh.' When I looked up, he cocked his head back with eyes wide open, gave me a toothy smile, and rewarded me with a happy laugh, his first. Of course, I laughed too. I can just imagine how Chinese intonations with a Southern accent must have sounded."

Summer and Shift Rotations

Summer evenings and nights took on new meaning as the nursing students began shift changes. They worked a shift—either 4:00 p.m. to midnight or midnight to 8:00 a.m.—for ten days and then switched to a new shift. Janet recalls the difficulty of shift changes and losing weight because her eating and sleeping habits were disrupted. "During this time in particular, I realized this was the life of a nurse, and I could better see the responsibility and challenges involved in total patient care."

They were responsible for more patients on the ward and worked directly with the RN in charge of that shift. "My instructor assigned me patients about whom I received and gave reports at the change of shifts," Bette says. "In general, we were involved in more routine activities, such as preparing the patient for tests or procedures, and we were gaining more insight into functions of a hospital as a whole. I think this orientation was comprehensive enough to start working in a hospital upon graduation, yet many of us were told by staff nurses that we were not getting enough experience compared to the number of shifts they worked while in nursing school. This issue, in particular, seemed to trigger discussion over the quality of our educational program."

Janet was initially assigned the 4:00 p.m. to midnight shift. "This was a busy time with patients returning from treatments and surgery. We served dinner, gave nighttime medications, and prepared the patients for sleep by tightening the bedsheets, refilling water, and giving relaxing back rubs. The midnight to 8:00 a.m. shift began quietly, but still with many duties. We tried not to awaken patients unnecessarily when we checked on them each hour during the night, so we used a flashlight to check on patients and to take vital signs if ordered by the physician. The busiest time started around 4:00 a.m., when we began preparing patients for procedures or early surgery. Prior to breakfast, we recorded vital signs on all patients, gave patients a warm mini bath to wash their faces and hands, and repositioned them in bed so they were ready for their meal and to begin their daily care."

Janet became even more aware of the emotional needs of the patients during this time. "A lonesome feeling at night could be soothed by a nurse's gentle back rub, and a nurse's explanation could allay some of the fear and show the patient that someone understood," she says. "I also saw how much patients loved to see a bright smile and hear a 'good morning' after a seemingly endless dark, lonely, and perhaps painful night. I learned that holding the hand of a patient was an important gesture of caring and the importance of taking time with family members to discuss a patient's progress and how they could help with recovery. This would be the true life of a nurse—compassion and understanding along with skilled care."

Winnie spent the first part of summer rotation on a medical unit caring for a chronically ill patient, ultimately handling her death and the interaction with her family. "I also spent much time trying to observe lumbar punctures and prove to myself that I would not faint again," she recalls. Winnie had fainted when observing this procedure for the first time and was quite mortified to be rolled in a wheelchair and put to bed on the unit. "Having Dean Kemble come to see me in bed just made me more embarrassed. I questioned my ability to become a nurse at that point."

Night duty on the private medical unit was a challenge, particularly when, for a couple of nights, Winnie was assigned to be the charge nurse. This provided an opportunity to develop the leadership skills needed to manage a unit. "I remember feeling the responsibility heavily and trying desperately not to get sleepy around 4:00 a.m. I was always glad to see the sun rise with no mishaps having occurred."

Donna recalls the change of pace that came with staying up all night and not being as busily engaged with patients since they were mostly sleeping. "The most compelling activity for me, and the one that was adrenaline driven, was the occasional emergency delivery. Otherwise, the hour between 4:00 and 5:00 a.m. was really long; however, I vividly remember seeing some resplendently beautiful sunrises that signaled the night shift would soon be over,"

The nighttime rotation also changed their daytime routine, as Donna recalls:

> Most of the time the day was nearly slept away and there seemed to be little time to do anything, but one day was unique. My date and I had gone to see an evening movie at the theater on Franklin Street, and we were going to get a bite to eat after the show before I went on duty. Alas, the show did not end until close to 10:00 p.m., our curfew time. We raced back to the dorm; I signed in and quickly changed into my uniform, ready for the night shift.
>
> Since we were officially allowed to leave the dorm and walk to the hospital, we went back to town for our bite to eat at Mouson's on Franklin Street. We walked in the door, and only two tables were occupied since it was so late. Two ladies sitting at one table looked up when I crossed the threshold. Need I say who one of them was? Dean Kemble was sitting up so straight she looked taller and said in a very formal voice, 'Good evening, Ms. Blair.' I noticed how blue her eyes were, and I responded like it was midafternoon rather than eleven at night. I was shocked to see the dean out so late at night and particularly at that place. They left while we were still eating, thankfully without a 'good-bye, Ms. Blair,' and I kept looking at my watch to be sure I would be back at the hospital before report. Punctuality was not an option.

The next day I had a command appointment with the dean. Distilling the discussion very simply, I should not have detoured to Mouson's en route to the hospital, and most particularly, I should not have been in uniform. I thought it ironic that I never once wore my uniform, white shoes, and stockings to any class on campus, and yet, the one time I was in town late at night when the dean should have been in bed, I walked straight into an enclosed space with no retreat, and she was looking directly at me. I received restriction for a month, during which my grades improved, as did my respect for the dean and her principles. Dean Kemble held the line. She was fair and held no grudges, and right was right.

Outpatient Department

The nursing students' clinical experience expanded to the hospital's Outpatient Department, where outpatients were seen in various clinics for prenatal and postnatal care, follow-up treatments, preventive health care, consultations, or referrals. During this experience, the nursing students saw a full circle of "continuity of care" for patients.

"While in the Outpatient Department I saw some mothers I had seen in the OB-GYN clinic for prenatal care and was with in the hospital when their babies were born," Bette says. "It was quite rewarding to see patients returning for postpartum care. Sometimes I saw them with other health team members—such as physicians, medical students, dietitians, or specialists—but I also saw them individually, to teach, make a home visit, give care, or start a referral if indicated. Patients in the diabetic clinic came for regular follow-up and were occasionally admitted to the hospital if their blood sugar levels were too high or unmanageable as an outpatient or if they had a complication such as a foot ulcer."

A bit of competition arose occasionally between medical and nursing students when the same patient or procedure was sought for learning purposes. "Guess who won? I was asked by medical students and physicians if we were trying to be doctors since we weren't going to be real nurses," Bette says. "Sometimes it felt as though we were sitting ducks, waiting to be dunked."

Joy recalls her first day in the Outpatient Department. "There I stood with my registration papers, excited about a new experience with a family of four. The mother was very tall, and the man unusually short. Each parent carried a child, but I couldn't tell the sizes or ages of the children. Soon they were settled in an examining room after waiting for several doctors to appear. The diagnostic mystery was solved after several doctors visited: The parents wanted to find out if it was safe and prudent to have another child since the father and both children had a type of achondroplasia (dwarfism) that was genetic. Sometime later, I returned to Chapel Hill for a football game; down on the field were the UNC cheerleaders, attired in bright Carolina blue and white. One of them was a diminutive, precious little girl, jumping, dancing, and yelling her head off for her team, and I realized it was indeed their daughter."

One day while they were in the Outpatient Department, a massive thunderstorm knocked out all the power in the hospital. Dean Kemble praised the nursing students for helping during the big storm. The elevators were not working, and Bette worked in the kitchen, putting food on plates, then onto trays for students and others to carry to patients on various floors. Joy was assigned to do a catheterization on a female patient without any illumination except for candlelight and flashlights. "This would be my second catheterization, and I could easily miss the mark," she recalls. "But with good aim and lots of luck, I was successful. The head nurse was very pleased."

Polio: From Epidemic to Vaccine

In the early 1950s serious polio epidemics were increasing. Communities feared this disease, and any outbreak brought closure to swimming pools, theaters, and other crowded venues, even football games. Polio was a mysterious and devastating disease that often left long-term debilitating effects, and it seemed to target mostly young people.

"A pre-medical student who was in my freshman English class was now hospitalized with polio," Bette says. "He went on to medical school with his crutches, later becoming a psychiatrist. In April of 1955 came the announcement of a polio vaccine—the Salk Vaccine. A physician on our medical school research staff for whom I babysat a few times participated in the research with Dr. Jonas Salk."

Polio can paralyze muscles in the chest, requiring patients to use a breathing machine known as the iron lung. This airtight, cylindrical steel chamber enclosed a person's body except for the head and neck. The controlled pressure inside the chamber pulled air in and out of the lungs of patients who could not breathe independently. The iron lung was later replaced by the positive-pressure ventilator, which is the primary technology used today for patients who can't breathe on their own.

One night Bette was assigned to a fairly young woman with bulbar polio that had paralyzed her respiratory system. She "lived" in an iron-lung bed in a single room down a one-way hall. Everything physically done for her was accomplished through arm portholes situated around her tank respirator, but only after putting on gloves and an isolation gown. Bathing, changing her bed linen or gown, or moving her position were all done inside the iron lung. Nighttime can be scary for someone totally dependent on a machine for breathing. Fewer people are around to help or even to be seen in the hallway, and the hospital is quieter and generally darker. All night she pushed her signal light, and

Bette responded by going to her room to reposition a leg, arm, foot, or shoulder or to give her a drink of water.

"I answered her light every time, understanding her feeling of helplessness and her need to be with someone," Bette says. "As the hours of 5:00 to 7:00 a.m. approached, I fussed a little to the RN working with me, saying I couldn't get to my other duties because of being with this patient like a private duty nurse all night. I felt bad saying it, but later I was glad I did because it meant the RN was aware of my efforts. At the morning report, my instructor, Ms. Sump, told me the patient reported that I had neglected her. I explained the real events, and having an eyewitness didn't hurt. Ms. Sump immediately perceived the entire situation, which is one of the reasons for writing about this particular patient. She was there for me and for the patient."

Donna had a patient who was from her high school and just a class behind her. Donna entered his hospital room with trepidation. "He was in an iron lung, totally helpless; only his head was exposed. I was so taken aback with the size and loud rhythmic swooshing sound of the iron lung that I momentarily stopped breathing myself. It soon became routine, and my breathing became synchronous with his and the machine. I learned the difference between empathy and sympathy that semester, and I never experienced as intensive a work situation, as he slowly progressed from being in the iron lung to the rocking bed, where gravitational forces assisted his breathing. His girlfriend came over to Chapel Hill to visit a time or two followed by, sadly, 'the breakup.'"

Donna's high school classmate recovered and could walk with two canes. He could drive his car, which was reconfigured for driving with his hands only. "On several occasions he drove his car, packed with student nurses, as we all went out to eat at our favorite place, The Pines, owned by Janet's parents, Mr. and Mrs. Merritt," Donna recalls. "They were welcoming stand-in parents for the rest of our class, and we always gathered at The Pines for reunions in the coming years.

Joy and Geri Go to New York

In summer of 1954, Joy and Geri went to New York City. "That summer, we were all thinking about graduation the following June," Geri recalls. "My dream was to be an airline stewardess and travel to exotic places all over the world. Airlines wanted the stewardess staff to be nurses. (I would have been mortified if Dean Kemble ever heard anything about that plan.)"

Geri convinced Joy, who was her roommate at the time, to go with her to New York City and attend the John Robert Powers School of Modeling during the short vacation they had before beginning fall classes. "We stayed at Hotel Seville on Twenty-Second and Madison," recalls Geri.

Joy was going to interview with the airlines as well, but when her father found out about her venture in New York City, he telephoned long distance and said, "Joy, dear, I have spent all this time and money to send you to nursing school and to think that now you might be a *cocktail* waitress." Joy said, "I never tried anything like that after Daddy gave me that lecture!"

Donna was also in New York, bidding farewell to her parents, who were sailing to France for their first European trip. One more event that may have given Joy's father a jolt was when Joy accompanied Donna and her parents to the port, where they boarded the Holland American's Maasdam cruise ship to bid them farewell and wave as they embarked.

"Mother took Joy up to the top deck, where a reporter was taking pictures and write-ups of the passengers to send to their hometown papers," Donna recalls. "Joy was interviewed and had her picture taken for a write-up about her sailing to France that appeared in a Charlotte newspaper. I believe that Joy was able to call her parents long distance before it went to press, but the rest of the Charlotte readers didn't get that message."

Geri had met Bob Laport, her future husband, earlier that summer when he came to Chapel Hill to visit his childhood friend from New Jersey, Andy Williams. The weekend that Joy and Donna went aboard the Maasdam, Geri traveled to Greenwood Lake, New Jersey, with Bob and his family.

"As it turned out, Bob would take care of my travel plans for future years," says Geri. "He did a lot of driving between Glenn Ridge, New Jersey, and UNC during our senior year. Five days after June 6, 1955 (graduation for both of us but from different schools), Bob and I were married at Chapel of the Cross in Chapel Hill."

5

Senior Year

Senior year arrived at last. The fall semester of 1954 brought new experiences as the nursing students worked in the Outpatient Department in Chapel Hill, a small hospital in Smithfield, or an assigned public health department. Winnie remembers that senior year brought quite a change because it was the first time they did not see each other daily.

"Unlike my freshman year, when I felt less prepared and less certain about making it at Carolina, I now felt confident and ready for my last chapter in becoming a UNC nurse," Bette says. "Having plowed, planted, and nourished my right stuff, the people who were key during this final step were also key in my future nursing career."

Martha was married during her senior year and lived off campus, but before marrying Robert S. Cline, she had to take the big step of getting Dean Kemble's permission. "She produced awe and fear in both my husband to be and me," Martha recalls. Her future husband said, "I didn't worry as much about going to Martha's father for permission to marry as the trip to Dean Kemble." Dean Kemble gave her permission and a blessing and a bit of advice: "Be sure he does an equal share of the housework. I don't want my student flunking out because of that."

"Little did I know how much my nursing education—the public health experiences, visiting with sick, low-income families, and working in rural hospitals—would prepare me for my future life," she says.

In 1954, Arlene married Fredrick L. Thurstone, who had received a physics degree from UNC in 1953. She took a leave from the program around graduation time to give birth to their first child. Classmates visited, brought flowers, and celebrated with her in the hospital. Arlene went on to graduate in 1956.

The seniors felt an increasing need to express themselves. When presented with a revision of the dorm rules/regulations for the four nursing classes, they noticed that the senior and junior classes had identical rules. "We wanted our rules to match those of other senior coeds living in campus dorms. As the newly elected senior class president, I was to present the request to Dean Kemble," Bette says.

"To make an appointment to meet with the dean, I had to speak to associate professor of nursing and administrative assistant to the dean, Ms. Dalrymple, and with my classmates' and my collective anger I explained the situation to her. She listened and suggested that with the dean, I would get farther with honey than with vinegar."

"While in the dean's office, I saw four words, each beautifully decorated and individually framed, on her wall. The words *faith*, *work*, *play*, and *love* certainly showed her desire for balance," Bette says. Thanks to her perseverance, the seniors received senior rules. "Sometimes, all you have to do is ask—properly." One social rule that changed involved dormitory closing hours. Now, instead of both juniors and seniors sharing the same closing hours in the school of nursing dormitory, seniors had extended closing hours.

By the beginning of her senior year, Sally and her boyfriend, John, were very serious about each other. While Sally and Joy were in Salisbury doing their public health rotation, John was scheduled for chest surgery in Atlanta. Sally's request to leave and travel to Atlanta was denied. "It snowed on the day I had asked to leave, and the public health experience was canceled," she recalls. "I was so mad."

The Friday after Sally came back to Chapel Hill from Salisbury, she left for Atlanta to see John. On Monday she was expected to report for duty at the hospital. "The trip back was rushed, to say the least," Sally remembers. "I had rolled up my aggressively straight hair at the bus station in Atlanta. When I got back to Chapel Hill, I raced to the dorm, threw on my uniform, and headed to the unit."

Sally was assigned to a critical-care patient who was in an iron lung. "And who was that patient? Yes, it was Dean Kemble's good friend!" The pressure was really on, and Sally was so intensely occupied with the constant care and monitoring of vital signs that she didn't have an opportunity to stop the delivery of nursing care through the iron lung's upper-access portholes. Complicating the care even more, the patient had undergone cranial surgery as well.

"As I looked up, Dean Kemble and the patient's brother entered the room, toward the foot of the iron lung," Sally recalls. "Taking in everything, Dean Kemble stopped abruptly at the foot, where a brown paper bag marked 'HAIR' was taped onto the iron lung. Dean Kemble was quite disturbed when she saw the bag and marched out of the room to tell the head nurse to take me out of there. However, the head nurse told Dean Kemble that she wasn't in charge of Sally but that her instructor, Patty Lewis, was in charge."

The bag contained the patient's hair, which had been saved after the patient's head was shaved in preparation for cranial surgery. At this time, families wanted to keep the hair to use for the funeral preparation if the patient expired. Hospital procedure was to tape the bag of hair to the foot of bed, but a less obvious location for the bag might have been wise and less upsetting to Dean Kemble and the brother of the patient.

Dean Kemble was so upset that she did not come back to the hospital room. A few years later when Sally returned to Chapel Hill for an alumni meeting, Patty Lewis told her that after this occurrence, she had visited Dean Kemble's office and asked the dean if she wanted *her* job. The upshot of that was Dean Kemble said something to the effect that she didn't believe she would resign as dean.

Public Health Experiences

The fall semester took the students off campus to focus on community nursing in courses designed by Mrs. Gifford, who was a professor of nursing and the head of the Department of Community Nursing. An eight-week course provided supervised field practice in public health departments around North Carolina. This was possible through a collaboration between the School of Nursing and six counties selected for the training program.

Another community nursing course took them, four at a time, to the Johnston Memorial Hospital in Smithfield, North Carolina, for four weeks. These courses with field experiences gave the students awareness of the public health needs of North Carolina and its people.

This program of community health courses and affiliations certified the students for entry as level II public health nurses upon graduation. The Public Health Program was required for obtaining National League of Nursing accreditation, and when the school received national nursing accreditation in the fall of 1955, it became the only nursing school in North Carolina to achieve national accreditation. No other school in the state had a public health/community nursing program at that time, but since then home health and community health programs have increased exponentially.

Rae and Bette were assigned to the Forsyth County Health Department in Winston-Salem. "Newspaper headlines on October 6, 1954, announced our participation, and the health department staff went out of their way to help us," Bette says. "Two sisters who worked there offered us a place to live. They even gave us a ride to and from work. Their lovely home sat at the top of a steep hill in a desirable section of Winston-Salem, only a few blocks from restaurants and shops. Our upstairs bedroom with twin beds was decorated for two princesses, and that is how they treated us. Occasionally we visited with them in the living room or were invited for a meal."

Bette recalls that her field advisor, Ms. Marian Duggins, was experienced and astute in teaching. "When observing my work, she noted my strengths or limitations in specific areas of public health nursing," Bette says. "One of my cases was an eighty-three-year-old patient receiving bedside care biweekly in his home. Before visiting, I read an October 1954 article in the *American Journal of Nursing* that discussed the care of the aged in the home. The family in this home could use everything I learned from that article, and I learned from them too. The patient gave me a poem he had written on aging, and I shared the *Leaves of Gold* book of poems, asking him to pencil mark the ones he liked." Bette presented this family as a case study to the health department and later at the School of Nursing before a small group of faculty and school supporters at a luncheon at The Carolina Inn. "Today, with an increasing number of people living longer, we are focusing on the aged client in home—aging in place—more than ever. What I learned is as pertinent today as it was then," she says.

Janet spent the first two months of the semester with Gloria, Pat, and Donna in Greensboro at the Guilford County Public Health Department. "Each of us had a public health nurse for a mentor, and we eventually worked part of her territory ourselves," Janet recalls. "My assignment was a low-income apartment complex. I especially enjoyed the new mothers with infants, mothers with sick children, and the homebound elderly patients. The visits from the health nurses were well received, particularly by the elderly, who truly appreciated our care and concern for them. They often wanted to talk and tell stories of days gone by. I had many opportunities for teaching and to address health concerns and was rewarded to see how much the patient progressed after I shared information during my visit. Especially important was that I earned their friendship and respect. I enjoyed the public health experience because I had more interaction with patients in their own surroundings instead of only in a sterile hospital environment."

While in Greensboro they lived with a widow who owned a large home. "One night she left for a visit, and the house was all ours," Janet recalls. "We managed well until we heard noises, as if someone were trying to break into the downstairs. Of course we had no training in defense techniques, so my idea was to arm ourselves with razor blades and push the furniture in front of the bedroom doors. The only casualty turned out to be four sleepy nursing students the next day."

This experience was not only a clinical rotation but also a personal time of learning. Finding a place to live was a first for Donna. "As we looked for lodging, I learned the value of newspaper ads, networking, and dealing with terms of a contract," she says. "Cleo Osborne was assigned as my mentor, and I don't know whether our pairing was the result of a personality profile assessment or just the 'luck of the draw,' but Cleo was an ideal role model. She taught me the wide scope of practice for public health nursing and shared her wise counsel regarding decision making, responsibilities, and evaluating personal actions. I was with Cleo eight hours a day, five days each week, a truly unique one-to-one faculty-student ratio. Our usual routine was to go to the home office first thing in the morning to plan the day and then go into 'the field.' En route we stopped at what Cleo called the 'branch office,' code for the coffee shop where everyone seemed to know everyone else. Cleo's husband was a highway patrolman, and I became aware of the value of these public safety officers as it related to community welfare, particularly in a rural health setting."

The nursing students enjoyed football games and other activities on the weekends. One afternoon during their senior year, UNC alumnus Andy Griffith delivered his famous monologue, 'What It Was, Was Football' at a football game. "We were all spellbound hearing that Carolina mountain drawl on the loudspeaker as he portrayed the part of a 'country bumpkin' trying to figure out the game of football," Donna says.

On October 22, the circus was in Greensboro. Gwen remembers that her boyfriend, Dean, came to pick her up in Smithfield, and they pooled their money and drove back to Chapel Hill. "We caught a bus to Greensboro and then took a cab to the circus, where we met Gloria and Don," Gwen said. "By the time we bought our tickets for the circus, we were broke. My parents were supposed to be at the circus and then take us to our home in Thomasville afterward. Well, when we went into the tent, there were hundreds of people, and I thought, 'Oh, no. We will never find them.' We found a seat, and a short while later my dad came down the steps to us. They were just a few rows behind us. Whew!"

Gwen and Virginia lived in a private home during their public health rotation at the Gaston County Health Department in Gastonia. "The first night our landlady locked us out because we were later than she expected," Gwen remembers. "We kept knocking on the door until she let us in. That was a lesson learned. We had the opportunity to teach new mothers how to nurse and bottle-feed their new babies. This was difficult for the mothers and for us. The mothers were poor and not well educated. They were not in the learning mode."

Mary and Sara also spent time in Gastonia, where a local newspaper article announced their arrival. "The blue uniform dresses were worn with small navy hats to command respect," Mary says. In a later local newspaper article, Sara is quoted as saying, "These uniforms we wear do look like service-women's uniforms. We've been saluted several times."

Winnie and Louise were assigned to the public health agency in Concord. "My most memorable experience was my first solo visit to the country, driving the county van," Winnie recalls. "I got stuck and had to be pulled out by a tractor. Obviously, I returned late to the department, with everyone anxiously waiting. These experiences continued to broaden our views of families coping with difficult home situations and limited resources."

Rural Hospital Experience

During their rural hospital experience in Smithfield, the students lived in the nurses' residence with the other nurses at the Johnston

Memorial Hospital. Their orientation included working directly with nursing staff, families, and community resources in a setting more similar to other hospitals in North Carolina than to the teaching hospital in which they had been working. Gloria remembers that they were used to always having a resident, intern, or RN within calling distance, but in Smithfield, they were on the floor with the staff and learned to make decisions quickly. "We were expected to work a forty-four-hour week like the graduate nurses," Mary says.[5]

The patients had less complicated medical and surgical procedures than the students had experienced at North Carolina Memorial Hospital. "We observed tonsillectomies, appendectomies, and a few more basic surgeries we had not seen," says Janet. "For more specialized care, the patients were referred to UNC, Duke, or other larger facilities. This was a very pleasant experience for me. Patients brought us homemade goodies, as they enjoyed our care and friendship with them."

Gloria remembers coming in late one evening after working in the hospital. "I could not open the door to my room," says Gloria. "Bette had put Vaseline on the doorknob, and of course, it was very slippery. I got even with her somehow." Bette recalls that earlier that day after working the day shift, she returned to her room and a greased doorknob. "Thinking it was either one or both of my classmates next door who had done this, I returned the mischief." Bette says. "It took another day or so to discover that it was a hospital staff nurse, also living in the nurses' residence, who put the Vaseline on my door, thinking it would be a fun prank."

The slower working pace in Smithfield gave the student nurses much more time to attend to their assigned patients. "I cared for a middle-aged lady over a period of days," Donna recalls. "One day when I walked into her room, sitting by her bed was a glamorous woman who looked up with a dazzling and friendly smile. She was my patient's daughter. Over the next few days that hospital room became a gathering place as this model from New York demonstrated to the nurses how to put on eye makeup and to contour the face with powders and rouge. Alas, no powders could disguise or conceal my myriad freckles, but who would have thought that such a valuable lifetime lesson would be learned in a small rural hospital?"

Another unforgettable memory for Donna began one night on the evening shift. "A retired couple from New Jersey was en route to Florida when a car collision abruptly changed their plans. After they were treated in the ER, they were sent to our floor and were both admitted to the same double room. They argued intensely for the next twenty-four hours about why they had the wreck and whose fault it was. A care-plan reassessment called for a therapeutic separation. The wife (in her own room) became my patient for the next several days. I looked forward to caring for her and listening to her stories. In the course of the days of care she asked me about myself, and I told her that I had just become engaged and was getting married in February with the caveat that I would not move to Germany until after I graduated in May and took state boards in early June. The next morning, when I entered her room with an armload of fresh towels, sheets, and other supplies for the morning bath, she tried to give me some money. It so took me by surprise, and thoughts of Dean Kemble and professional ethics immediately flashed across my mind. After thanking her for her kind and generous thoughts, I said, 'I can't accept any money,' followed by, 'It would not be professional.' She made some kind of a 'hissing' or 'sissing' noise through her teeth and said with commanding authority, 'This isn't *money*! This is a *wedding gift*!' To this day I still have my very first wedding gift—the age-softened envelope holding those very same seven dollars."

Hurricane Hazel came to Smithfield during Gwen's time there. "The ward room in the hospital had long windows, so we could see the storm coming. We stayed at the hospital. There was no power overnight except for the generator. We had no elevator and no stove for cooking, so we carried cold meals up and down the stairs to the patients. A taxi driver stayed outside the emergency room in case a doctor was needed. He would drive to the doctor's office and tell him the message."

Winnie was also in Smithfield during Hurricane Hazel. "We were awakened early and told we had to help cover the floors since some of the staff would be unable to get into work," she remembers. "I remember being on auxiliary power, with dim lights and no elevators. If patients—or bodies—had to be transported, they were carried manually down the stairs. We rose to the occasion and did our part."

Spring Semester

By spring semester the nursing students were back in Chapel Hill. "Spring was a beautiful blur of adventures," Gwen recalls. "Our classes were preparing us for futures as graduate nurses. The completion of our four years was nearing, and we were grasping for any amount of knowledge we may have missed. My sister, Gloria, was married in April, and we had several parties in preparation for her big day. Of course, we went to football and basketball games in our spare time. The football team was terrible the entire four years, but watching the basketball team was more fun and more exciting."

Bette remembers taking five courses, two of which were on main campus—the Negro (Sociology 125) and the Origin and Significance of the Bible (Religion 28). She had her first African American teacher for the course on "the Negro." "He was comfortable presenting a comprehensive understanding of facts and myths from the past and present about his culture and life in our country," she says. "The movement in America in support of inclusion of African Americans was slowly growing. I became an active participant for change over the next sixty years.

"I took the Bible as an elective instead of economics, thinking it would not be as difficult. It wasn't easy, but it was enlightening," Bette says. "I learned that the Bible contained different versions of the same stories in different chapters, depending on the author. I grew up listening to the same Bible stories read to me, not directly reading them. I was familiar with The Book of Common Prayer and its precise selections for each Sunday and religious observations but had not realized its limitations. By my senior year, I had changed—issues that were formerly black and white were now vaguely gray. I relied more on developing my own thinking and sense of beliefs."

Sally and her roommate, Martha, had started smoking during their freshman year. They would buy a pack of cigarettes, cut the cigarette in two, and then hold it with a bobby pin to smoke it because it was so short and got hot. By the time she was a senior, Sally was smoking a whole cigarette.

They all had brand-new beds with a thick mattress that rested on a board atop two large storage drawers. One day, Donna was teaching Sally to knit argyle socks, and the two of them sat on Sally's bed practicing between classes. Then, Donna left Sally to knit and crossed the hall to her room.

"Everyone knew that Sally could really concentrate, and this surely was one of those times," recalls Donna. "The intricate pattern and the bobbins really did take concentration, and Sally dropped her cigarette on the bed right beside her and kept knitting away."

After a while Donna and Sara smelled smoke and went out into the hall and directly to Sally's room. "She was gone, and the bed was smoking," Donna says. After class, Sally came back to her room to find a new mattress on the bed. "I was so scared because I thought I would get kicked out of school, but no one even mentioned the incident until many years later."

In 1965, Sally returned to Chapel Hill as part of the School of Nursing faculty. During Dean Kemble's orientation class for new faculty members, she laughingly told the tale. She said that the faculty didn't mention the incident when it happened because "she was such a good little child."

Comprehensive Nursing

At midcentury, hospital admissions were increasing, and patients received care from medical and nursing teams rather than from a specific physician. The nursing team—RNs, LPNs, nursing aides, and orderlies—was part of the broader health-care team.

Ms. Esther Sump taught the comprehensive nursing class that prepared the nursing students for leadership on a nursing team and in developing patient-centered care plans. "I am incredibly fortunate to have had her as my teacher," Bette says.

During the clinical experiences for this class, the head nurse led the nursing staff, and a student would function as a team leader, planning and organizing each patient's care and delegating work for members on the team. "This involved taking into consideration the physical, social, psychological, and medical orders for individual patients," Bette recalls. "For example, I cared for a woman whose husband was suspected of slowly poisoning her with arsenic. Besides helping her to recover from devastating loss of functioning, every person involved in her care had to behave in an unsuspicious manner when with her or her husband, as each aroused a different set of feelings. It looked like we were dealing with a criminal case, and investigators were part of the scenario, so the husband could not be left alone in the room with her. That took a lot of maneuvering and team effort."

Bette also cared for a young teenage bride of a military groom. She was admitted shortly after their honeymoon because of an elongated clitoris. "In a teaching hospital, the unusual is displayed for teaching purposes, so many came to look," Bette says. "It was a bewildering experience for our patient, her husband, and her parents. It was a challenge to coordinate privacy and respectful care."

That semester the School of Nursing expected site visits from the North Carolina Board of Nurse Examiners as part of the process with the National League for Nursing to achieve accreditation and become the first school in the state with full accreditation from this organization.

Donna remembers being surprised one morning as Dean Kemble approached her on the floor in the hospital. "Her posture was always erect, and whether standing, walking, or sitting, her back was straight. In midheels and wearing a lab coat, she informed me that she and the nurse examiner from the state would observe me that morning while I performed a catheterization on my patient. There was little time to think about the impact of this procedure, so I just proceeded to get the tray and explain to the patient what I would be doing and why. I was rather surprised that I felt so calm, but it happened so quickly I didn't have time to think of any negative possibilities."

Dean Kemble and the nurse examiner were at the bedside opposite Donna, which was good since she was left-handed and could comfortably carry out the required draping and mandated sterile technique. "Dean Kemble was remarkable and highly professional; she made not only me, but also my patient, feel at ease," Donna says. "She spoke to the patient in a friendly, conversational tone, smiled easily, and engaged the examiner in conversation as well. Most fortunately for me, my patient's exposed anatomy was in the exact place where it was supposed to be. This was fortuitous, since it was my first catheterization. Most importantly, our school received accreditation in the fall of 1955."

Donna says that she never saw Dean Kemble in a nursing uniform—cap, pin, white shoes, and hose. "I can only imagine how she was before she was 'The Dean,' when she was Elizabeth Kemble, RN, on duty in a hospital somewhere in Ohio or New York wearing her crisp white uniform and nursing cap, interacting with and caring for patients, and setting the standard for excellence in professional nursing. The bar would be very high indeed."

Psychiatric Rotation

The North Carolina Memorial Hospital's Psychiatric Department was housed in a new, separate building next to the main hospital. It had two inpatient units—one with unlocked doors and the other with locked doors for more serious patients—and also housed outpatient units, offices, and areas for patient activities. Patients had individual psychotherapy with a psychiatric resident and also participated in group therapy on the ward.

"It was a different world for me when I was introduced to psychiatric nursing, taught by Ms. Barbara Bernard, an expert on the subject," Bette recalls. "The patients were unlike any I had seen before, since this was my first exposure to persons in psychotic states. The new words and diagnoses were challenging—schizophrenia, obsessive compulsive disorder, manic depressive, psychosis, neurosis, unconscious ego-defense mechanisms, and so on. Today, there is a greater understanding of the role of genetics in mental illness and better treatments for the two primary illnesses affecting mood and thought."

At that time, psychiatric group therapy was fairly new in the United States. A visiting British psychiatrist introduced group therapy and worked with the psychiatric staff and patients to implement this new approach. "I liked that nurses were part of the psychiatric team that developed therapeutic plans for each patient," Bette says.

"Our hospital was implementing a new treatment with patients," Janet says. "There was an open-door policy, which allowed patients out of their rooms to walk, take part in activities in the dayroom, and interact with other patients."

The nursing students attended teaching rounds, during which a faculty psychiatrist interviewed patients. "Dr. Bernard Glueck was a favorite of mine and many others," Bette says. "He was a famous older psychoanalyst who had been analyzed by Sigmund Freud, and it was marvelous to see patients undergo some positive change just while being therapeutically interviewed by him." *The Catcher in the Rye* by J. D. Salinger had just been published in 1951 and was recommended reading for some of the inpatient adolescents.

Donna notes that the psychodynamics were fascinating. "I wished that we had more clinical time and could have attended the physicians' grand rounds and conferences," she says. "At that time the culture of the hospital was more hierarchical, and those opportunities were not available, particularly for nursing students."

Donna remembers that one of her patients was a thin, raw-boned navy veteran, about forty years old, who was catatonic. "I first saw him when I walked in the large, open dayroom where the patients gathered for leisure, games, or some loosely organized activity and could still be observed by staff from a glass-enclosed nursing station. He looked like a statue sitting in a straight chair, feet flatly planted on the floor, both hands rigidly clutching an open Bible across his lap while staring unblinkingly in the distance. Nothing and no one evoked the slightest reaction during the entire morning, and when I left 'clinical' at noon, he was still frozen in that position. Little did I know that Ms. Bernard would assign him to be my next patient.

"I cared for him after his initial electroshock treatment," Donna says. "He was lying on his back when I went to the bedside to check his vital signs. Then he suddenly lunged over and grabbed me around my knees with both arms in a viselike grip. I could not believe what had just happened. It was like a coiled strike—lightning fast. In a nanosecond I processed that I could either call for help or try to quietly deal with it myself. Since he didn't make the slightest further move, I elected to try to pry his arms from my knees—with absolutely no success. He seemed to be frozen in a catatonic grip. What saved the day was that the door to his room was wide open. A very tall, lean doctor in a long lab coat walked by, glanced in, stepped backward, did a double take, and took the longest four strides to the bedside. Between the two of us we were able to dislodge his arms from the crush of my (by now very wrinkled) white, starched apron. My patient slowly began to improve. One day, with a furrowed brow and the most distraught and riveting look, he pointedly murmured, 'I didn't know I was crazy,' almost as if it was a question. The history on the chart stated that when he disembarked from his ship in San Francisco he went to a bar and 'got rolled.'"

Among several patients assigned to Bette, her case study was a young man in his late teens diagnosed with schizophrenia. "He hallucinated, was delusional, avoided contact with others, and received messages from the television set," Bette says. "Medications included some of the first antipsychotics (Thorazine and Mellaril), which are rarely or never used today. During my time on the psychiatric ward I saw little improvement in him, didn't really understand his condition, and was unable to establish a relationship with him."

During the psychiatric rotation, the class took a field trip to Dorothea Dix Hospital, the state psychiatric institution in Raleigh. "There we observed the more traditional treatment for mental illness:

electrical shock treatment, or EST as it was often called," Janet recalls. "This was the most traumatic treatment I recall. This hospital was not a pleasant setting, although I am certain many patients were helped at that time by this standard practice."

At Dorothea Dix Hospital, some of the nursing students delivered dinner trays to patients in solitary rooms. "I took a tray and walked down a long hall to a patient's room," recalls Donna. "The bottom of the locked door had an open slit approximately six inches in height and wide enough to slide the tray through. On my hands and knees, I slid the tray in. When I looked through the slit, I was jolted to see the face of a beautiful young black girl with perfect teeth grinning at me on the other side of the door. Her big brown eyes were flashing, and she never blinked, almost like a cat watching a mouse before a swift and certain pounce. When she saw my reaction, she just started laughing hysterically. I was so shocked and felt so foolish that I started laughing too. It was contagious. Her hearty and wonderfully deep, infectious laugh made me laugh even more. It seemed like we were taking turns laughing until my eyes began watering and my sides hurt—I absolutely had to pull away and get back to the group. She kept laughing as I crawled out of her line of vision. I was breathless and amazed with the whole encounter. I obviously had a lot to learn about psychiatric nursing. She was just one of the hundred-plus patients at Dix Hill. One of the many things I learned that day is that a type of schizophrenia called hebephrenic schizophrenia is characterized by senseless laughter, delusions, foolish mannerisms, and a severe disintegration of personality."

Another memorable experience for Donna occurred during her introduction to occupational therapy (OT). "The OT department was on the first floor in a large room with tables and chairs, looms, easels, paints, and crafts all around," she says. "Outside was a large grassy area where the patients could participate in outdoor activities. A brick wall probably ten or twelve feet tall enclosed this area. I was asked to stay outside with a group of patients who were mostly just meandering around enjoying the sun. We had been there for about ten minutes, when I saw a sudden flash of activity. As I swung my head toward the action, I caught sight of a tall, lanky black teenager as he hit the wall midstep, halfway up, grabbed the ledge, and leaped over. The patients and I froze, dumbfounded. It was astounding and so quiet. When it sunk in, I realized that I was the only one outside who was not a patient, and I had to go inside to report the incident. I hurried toward the door and glanced back, almost afraid to leave the rest of the group for fear someone else would try it. Just as I looked back, here he came, flying back over the wall again, landing on his feet. It was such a surprise, but I had to smile and breathe a sigh of relief—all's well that ends well."

Bette had no interest in pursuing psychiatric nursing at the time and was just happy to have it behind her. "Later in my nursing career, I became a psychiatric clinical nurse specialist and was part of the first group of nurses to become certified by the American Nurses Association (ANA)," she says.

Face to Face with Dean Kemble

The spring semester included the senior seminar, during which the sixteen of them were in a small seminar, face to face with Dean Kemble, for a whole semester. "The dean's senior seminar was the most lasting and important course for my entire professional career," Bette says. Winnie says that having Dean Kemble as their instructor made them realize that they were closing in on the last leg of their journey. "As parents do, she was trying to prepare us for the launch," Winnie says. "She had truly been an awesome leader, disciplinarian, friend, and teacher. Her own demeanor and expectations set quite an example."

Dean Kemble started the class by asking if nursing was a profession. "The question had never occurred to me, although I would soon be a professional nurse—distinguishing myself from nonprofessional nurses," Bette says. She posed other questions too: What is the definition of a profession? How do you define nursing? And is nursing dependent on another profession (medicine) for its practice?

Dean Kemble encouraged good thinking and required one textbook to stimulate discussion: *American Nursing: History and Interpretation* by Mary M. Roberts, RN. The Macmillan Company published the book in July, 1954, and it cost six dollars. "The book raised the same thought-provoking questions posed by Dean Kemble, but during our seminar discussion, clarity on the topics took root," Bette says. A profession has its own identity, defines its own standards of practice, and is not dependent on another to define it. Nurses were more dependent than interdependent, and definitely not independent in practice, although today we have professional nurses who are independent practitioners. "Dean Kemble stressed the importance of being a member of the ANA and of supporting and improving the professional standing of nursing," Bette says.

Dean Kemble asked each student to write a paper on nursing. "I wrote on Florence Nightingale, who cleaned up hospitals, patients, and the environment; organized administration of nurses and services; and changed nursing into respectable work—proceeding to transform the practice of nursing into a profession," Bette says. "She is recognized as the founder of modern nursing and for her notable contributions to nursing theory and nursing practice. I liked writing about her, but stayed up all night finishing my paper."

Janet was somewhat apprehensive about this term paper and oral presentation. "We were required to make an oral presentation to the class and to Dean Kemble," Janet says. "The majority of our grade was based on this presentation. There was no doubt Dean Kemble wanted us to further our nursing careers into the educational area. Many of the girls chose to do just that."

Bette was surprised when the dean asked them to grade themselves and each classmate for her course. This was a seminar for senior students, and she treated them as such.

Activities

During their senior year, Donna and Geri had the honor of being invited to be members of the Order of the Old Well. Sally had become a member her junior year and served on the executive committee of the Order of the Old Well her senior year. The organization was founded during World War II, in 1943, to recognize students who demonstrated outstanding humanitarian services in various campus activities and who exhibited a willingness to perform functions that did not offer recognition.

"The Old Well is the most enduring symbol of UNC and is at the heart of the campus. It serves as part of the UNC logo and is thought to be as old as Old East Dormitory, dating from the 1790s," Donna says. The Old Well served as the sole water source for Old East and Old West Dormitories. It was redone in its current style in 1897 and given its present decorative style from the Temple of Love in the garden of Versailles. "It is said that if you drink from the Old Well on the first day of classes, you will have success for the semester. How I wish I had known that, when it was only a stone's throw away from Smith Dorm. I see a connection and similarity between the symbol of the Old Well and the symbol for nursing, Florence Nightingale's lamp. The Old Well represents education in general, and Florence Nightingale's lamp represents education in nursing, specifically. Both symbols are iconic, recognized, and enduring."

*Rae, Mary, Janet, Gloria, Gwen, Pat, Sara, Donna, Geri, Sally,
Virginia, and Bette attended Donna's wedding in February, 1955.*

At Christmas break Donna became engaged to Brantley C. Booe
Jr., now First Lieutenant Booe. "He was the man I knew I would marry," she says. "We had planned to marry after graduation; however,
in early January those plans were abruptly changed with the arrival
of Brantley's orders to report to Neubiberg Air Force Base in Munich,
Germany, on February 20, 1955. Thanks to my mother's organizational and planning capabilities, we married on February 12, 1955, in
Winston-Salem with most of my nursing classmates in attendance. It
was such a cold winter night that when Brantley tried to wipe off the
back window with 'JUST MARRIED' written in white shoe polish,
the rag froze on the window and stayed there until the next day, when
we returned to Chapel Hill and the temperature was higher.

Donna had to be on duty on the psychiatric floor Monday morning at 8:00 a.m. sharp. "My instructor was Ellie Soutsos, and as I was passing her in the hall, she addressed me as Mrs. Booe. I continued for a step or two before realizing that she was speaking to me," Donna recalls. "She had a great sense of humor, and we laughed about my lapse of remembering that I was now Mrs. Booe. At the end of the week Brantley left for Germany, and I began marking off each day on the calendar until graduation. Some days, but not many, the clock seemed to whip around in double time."

In the spring, Gloria was busy planning a wedding that would take place during Easter break. "We married before graduation because Don was in the ROTC and we knew he would be called at any time," she recalls. "How I passed the semester, I will never know. I helped Don write a paper on topography and made my wedding dress. We had Monday after Easter off from classes, but Don wanted me to have another day off from classes. I dared not ask Dean Kemble," Gloria says. They had already discussed their wedding plans with her, but Don would not be deterred. The two of them made an appointment with Dean Kemble, and Don told her why they would like to have an extra day for their honeymoon. "She looked at the two of us and said she would be fine with this," Gloria recalls. "I was shocked, but Don felt this was what she would say. We did marry in April, and I moved into his apartment. We settled in and studied hard until graduation."

---

[5] See a full copy of the rules for the nursing students at Johnston Memorial Hospital in Smithfield online at http://dc.lib.unc.edu/cdm/search/collection/nchh/searchterm/NCHH-123/order/identi.

6

Graduation and Licensing Exam

All of a sudden, the nursing students found themselves in a whirlwind of activities. As they prepared for graduation, they were feted and acknowledged as the first class of nurses to graduate from Carolina and the first graduates in the state to obtain a four-year bachelor of science in nursing. "We were quite proud," Winnie says.

As the end of their senior year approached, they decided to leave a gift to the school as their legacy. "The gift had to be very special, as we were the first graduating class," Janet says. "Dean Kemble had given so much to us and to the school, and we thought a portrait of her would be a permanent reminder of her contributions that could be enjoyed now and in years to come." They had some difficulty in attaining their goal. Dean Kemble had to be persuaded, and their bank account was not enough for the best oil painting, and they had to have the best, of course. The seniors created a fund that would continue each year until the goal was completed.

Having made it to graduation, several activities were scheduled for them to celebrate with others connected with this endeavor. They had a Coke party at Ms. Sump's home and dinner with Mrs. Brower, their dorm mother, at The Pines Restaurant.

One memorable event was a dinner on May 17, 1955, that Mrs. Spencer Love gave in her home for the sixteen students and representatives from the school and university. Mrs. Love was a member of Mrs. Elizabeth Carrington's School of Nursing Committee, which was formed in 1953 to make plans for securing much-needed funding for scholarships and to recruit new students. Mrs. Carrington was an RN with a master's degree from the University of Pennsylvania, and she tirelessly traveled the state raising funds for the School of Nursing. The outstanding work of this committee, which also included Dr. Lois Stanford, Ruth Wilson, Mary Ragsdale, Dean Kemble, and Dr. Frances Hill Fox, enabled the baccalaureate in nursing program to not just exist but to also have the funding and support to continually grow stronger, elevating the education of nurses in the state of North Carolina.

"Mrs. Love gave generously toward our education at the School of Nursing, and she was quite proud of this graduating class," says Janet. "In our formal wear, we were delighted with the evening and festivities. We will always remember this very special lady."

"Not only was it an honor meeting the people who played such an important role in the school; it was a festive occasion," Bette says.

After dinner, Mrs. Carrington spoke with Bette concerning her and Sara joining the School of Nursing faculty as assistant clinical instructors immediately after graduation. "I don't think you should go into the School of Nursing—get experience first," she advised. Bette did not take the advice.

The nursing students enjoyed attending a dinner at Mrs. Spencer Love's home. On floor: Bette, Geri, Gloria, Donna. Second row: Louise, Joy, Mary, Janet, Sally, Gwen, Rae. Third row: Martha, Virginia, Pat, Sara, Winnie.

Another graduation event for the class included a special senior-faculty breakfast on Friday, June 3, at The Carolina Inn. Each student received a program with the theme "After Four Years Dreams Come True." On the front cover was a photo of the class taken in 1951, and toward the back, a photo of them in 1955 in their nursing-student uniforms. Inside was the menu, the list of faculty speakers and Dean Kemble for the address, and a page for autographs. "Getting everyone to sign the autograph page was the most fun of all, and that page brings back many memories of people dear to us," recalls Bette.

Graduation

Graduation week arrived at last! "Formal invitations had been mailed for the weekend of June 4. Caps and gowns were distributed, we were given our schedules for the various social events and festivities, and family and friends arrived in Chapel Hill for the various teas, luncheons, and other festivities," Donna says.

Graduation at the UNC School of Nursing—Exercises in Honor of the Class of 1955—occurred at 3:30 p.m. on Monday, June 6, 1955, in the Nursing School Amphitheater. The graduation ceremony was followed by a tea reception in the Nursing Dormitory.

In their professional attire, seated: Louise, Martha, Pat, Janet, Gwen, Sally, Winnie. Standing: Joy, Rae, Geri, Bette, Donna, Sara, Virginia, Gloria, and Mary.

"We appeared in our professional attire for the first time—our crisp white uniforms, our caps, white stockings, and shoes," Janet recalls. "We received the final touch to complete the outfit, as each girl was individually called to receive our school pin, presented by Dean Kemble. We were now the nurses who began a journey four years ago. I can remember my mom and dad and how proud they were—their daughter had achieved her goal: to be a nurse."

As president of the senior class, Bette presented Dean Kemble with the class gift. "During the ceremony I told her that this class of 1955, the first graduating class of the University of North Carolina School of Nursing, decided to leave a portrait of the first dean of our school. However, due to the small membership in our class, our financial resources could not see our project materialized. Therefore, we are leaving a check of one hundred dollars to the UNC School of Nursing to begin a fund so that in the near future, subsequent donations will make it possible to have an oil painting of Dean Kemble, the first dean of the University of North Carolina School of Nursing."

At the tea reception in the Nursing Dormitory, "one food item was a slice of white bread without a crust and a white filling, then rolled into a scroll and tied with a Carolina-blue ribbon—an edible diploma," recalls Martha. Many photos were taken to show the graduates in their white uniforms and caps, and Dean Kemble gave each student a small two-by-three envelope with a folded, handwritten note.

Dean Kemble's note read: "Congratulations! And may God continue to bless you in all that you do."

For the university graduation, they gathered at the Old Well with all the other graduating students, dressed in black robes and caps for their honorary walk to Kenan Stadium. "The nursing students donned nursing's apricot-colored tassels for distinction from other degree programs," says Janet.

UNC president Gordon Gray gave special recognition to the first nursing class of UNC to receive a bachelor of science in nursing. They walked one at a time to the podium, where Governor Luther Hodges individually presented their diplomas. Chancellor Robert House presented each of them a Bible with an imprinted certificate inside containing his signature and the university seal. President Gordon Gray and Dean Elizabeth Kemble were also there to congratulate them. "Chapel Hill was my hometown, so many of my family and friends were in attendance, and as a result, I received quite an ovation when my name was called," Janet says. "As I walked across the stage, the smiling governor quipped: 'You have quite a fan club, it seems.' I returned his smile, thanked him, and graciously accepted my diploma with pride."

The speaker for the 161st Commencement Program for the University of North Carolina was the great American poet and three-time Pulitzer Prize winner Carl Sandburg. Sandburg was a native of Illinois who moved to Flat Rock, North Carolina, after the war in 1945.

Carl Sandburg was seventy-seven years old and had a full head of white hair and defined eyebrows. He was a prolific writer of not only poetry, but also prose, biographies, and children's books. His biography of Abraham Lincoln won him one Pulitzer Prize. His commencement speech was not long, but it was a distillation of what he had learned in his lifetime. He spoke of new developments in communications and technology and their effect on culture.[6]

"What I remembered was his tribute to the pioneers, to those who had the genius in their hearts to struggle and take hold," Donna says. "Dean Kemble was one of those. She was our pioneer who took the reins and struggled, in spite of obstacles and prevalent provincial attitudes, to successfully establish the state's first four-year baccalaureate-nursing-degree school at the University of North Carolina. My classmates and I were privileged to be the first graduates and charter members of her school. It is a pleasure and joy to know that the lamp is being passed to those nurses following us."

The class of 1955 graduated on June 6. Seated: Louise, Martha, Pat, Janet, Gwen, Sally, Winnie. Standing: Joy, Rae, Geri, Bette, Donna, Sara, Virginia, Gloria, Mary.

"As the ceremony ended, we shifted our apricot-colored tassels to the other side of our caps and realized a long journey had been completed: to achieve our bachelor of science in nursing from the University of North Carolina at Chapel Hill," Janet says.

After graduation, a group of them and their parents ate at the Rathskeller, also known as "The Rat." "My mom and dad enjoyed every moment of the day," Bette says.

"Our excitement and happiness is reflected in those pictures of student uniforms, graduate uniforms, and caps and gowns," Mary says. "A special treasure is the picture of our mothers, to whom we owed so much."

Licensing Examination

"There was much celebrating following the graduation ceremonies; however, amid all the fanfare, a small cloud still hung over our heads," says Janet. "Yes, the time had come to face the State Board of Nursing Examinations that would qualify us to be registered nurses. For four years we had studied and worked for this license."

After graduating on June 6, Geri married her husband, Bob, on June 11. They had a short honeymoon at Nags Head, and then returned to Raleigh for state board exams. Similarly, on June 9, Mary married James A. Leggette Jr., a graduate of the first class of the UNC School of Dentistry in 1954.

Like many of them, Winnie remembers Dean Kemble's words regarding passing the state boards. "When we approached her in the nursing seminar with a question of not passing boards, her answer was that it was not a matter of whether or not we would pass, but how well we would do," Winnie recalls. Gwen remembers Dean Kemble saying, "You will all pass your boards and do so with a 90 percent or above."

The North Carolina State Board of Registration Examination consisted of individual tests for nursing in medicine, surgery, obstetrics/gynecology, pediatrics, and psychiatry. "There were two days of testing, and the exams were as difficult as anticipated," Janet says. "Time was a factor—if you did not finish, you had to stop and your exam was collected. I was certain after not completing all the questions that there was cause for concern."

Don and Gloria moved to Windsor, North Carolina, after graduation. "I began work in the small community hospital and feel this truly helped me with my state boards," Gloria says. "We all dreaded taking the exam. We felt we would leave the country if we failed. Who could have ever faced Dean Kemble? The week following the boards was so nerve-wracking. Would the mail ever arrive, and how could we open the envelope? I believe Don opened mine for me; what a joy and a big relief!"

"When I did receive my scores, I discovered that I had done very well, as had the entire class," Janet says. "This success we could attribute to dedicated instructors, who instilled in us the knowledge and skills to be the best-trained nurses possible. Many thanks to these gifted ladies: Alice Gifford, Ruth Boyles, and Ruth Dalrymple from our beginning in Miller Hall, followed by Eloise Lewis, Esther Sump, Ruth Lindberg, Sylvia Kiger, Catherine Findlay, and Evangeline Soutsos. The rest of the faculty was chosen as time went by. Of course, they were all recruited by the best mentor possible, Dean Kemble, just as she had chosen all of us to begin the process with her. She inspired us with her wisdom, dedication, and determination to see her dream become a reality. I believe she admired our diligence and commitment to become registered nurses with college degrees."

"We realized with pride and confidence that there were unlimited avenues open to us for successful careers in nursing," Janet says. "We had achieved our goal. There is much to be said, however, of the journey rather than the destination. These seventeen kindred sisters who pioneered the course would now take separate paths in life, but would always share a bond with wonderful friendships to remember."

---

[6] Carl Sandburg's complete commencement address can be found on page 17 of the Fiftieth Anniversary *Yackety Yack*—Carolina Class of 1955.

7

Early Life after Graduation

After graduating and passing their boards the summer of 1955, the students went their separate ways. Several stayed in Chapel Hill after graduation, obtaining positions at the North Carolina Memorial Hospital or at the School of Nursing. Others moved to cities and towns across the Tar Heel State.

Gwen's husband was in pharmacy school at UNC Chapel Hill, so she started her career at North Carolina Memorial Hospital on a medical unit for private patients. She predominantly worked the 3:00 to 11:00 p.m. shift, but occasionally worked 11:00 p.m. to 7:00 a.m. "Working ten nights straight was exhausting, and it usually took the first two of the four days off to recover," Gwen remembers. "One day, one of the doctors had twins, and I was asked to do private duty for the twins for their first two nights—such fun."

Gwen worked at North Carolina Memorial Hospital until her husband graduated from School of Pharmacy in June, 1957, and they moved to Graham, North Carolina. "In anticipation of moving to Graham, I talked with a physician who had a private practice there. The only question he asked me was, 'Can you type?' Of course, I said yes and got the job. I couldn't help but wonder that I had four years of college and a BSN, and all he wanted to know was if I could type. I had taken typing in high school."

Gwen soon found out why he had asked about her typing ability. "There were no computers yet, so I did the billing and insurance papers while the other nurse assisted him. This was a good learning experience for me, and I was able to assist the doctor when the other nurse was off duty."

A year later Gwen and her husband moved to Lexington, North Carolina, where she worked in labor and delivery at a community hospital. "This was really different from Chapel Hill. As I was pregnant during this time, I learned the dos and don'ts of pregnancy before I delivered my first son."

They next moved to Valdese, North Carolina, where her husband worked in a local drugstore and Gwen worked at a hospital that had a nursing program. "I taught for a year and helped develop a new nursing program at Lenoir-Rhyne College. I enjoyed developing the program, but teaching nursing was not my forte."

In November of 1961, Gwen and her husband moved to Tryon, North Carolina, and purchased a local drugstore. "I stopped nursing for thirteen years to assist my husband in the pharmacy. This involved billing, buying merchandise, helping fill prescriptions, and making salads for the lunch fountain, all while raising four children."

On Monday, June 20, 1955, Mary began as a staff nurse at North Carolina Memorial Hospital, with a starting salary of $2,940 per year. "Newly married and working rotating shifts as my husband finished graduate work in orthodontics, my student days ended. I worked on 5 West, where Sue Ireland was head nurse, and then in the Outpatient Department headed by June Watson. That experience

Mary and her husband, December, 1955.

in the outpatient pediatric clinic stood me in good stead with my own children in later years."

Mary and her husband then moved to Durham, North Carolina, where her husband practiced orthodontics from 1956 to 1988. "My education was invaluable in my personal life as a mother of three children and wife to a professional man, and in volunteer work in the community."

Bette and Sara received appointments as assistant instructors in the School of Nursing Department of Clinical Nursing and began work on July 1. "I liked the idea of working with students and with Ms. Esther Sump in medical nursing, Ms. Ruth Lindberg in obstetrical nursing, and Ms. Beulah Gautefald in pediatrics," Bette says. Sara was assigned to be with Ms. Eloise Lewis in surgical nursing and Ms. Barbara Bernard in psychiatric nursing."

Although the annual salary was $3,000, about the same as a staff nurse at North Carolina Memorial Hospital, they didn't have to rotate shifts and had the weekends free. At this time, all faculty members were women. None were married or had children, and most were middle aged. One Saturday afternoon Bette ran into Dean Kemble at the post office. "She informed me that 'faculty members do not wear Bermuda shorts in public.'"

Bette assisted students with their clinical learning in the hospital and observed the faculty members organizing records and arranging final visits from the National League of Nursing. In the fall of 1955 the school received national nursing accreditation, becoming the first nursing school in North Carolina to have this distinction.

"Working with the faculty heightened my awareness of their hard work and dedication in the education of nursing students," Bette remembers. "It was good experience, but I missed working directly with patients and with other health-care providers."

After Ms. Dalrymple assured Bette that the next year working at the School of Nursing would be similar to her first, Bette decided she was ready to move on. Sara, too, resigned and explored Europe before beginning her next job.

Having gained some experience caring for medical and OB-GYN patients, Bette began working as a staff nurse in the psychiatric department of North Carolina Memorial Hospital. "It was uplifting to be part of a treatment team, directly contributing to care and participating in research studies. Working with a cadre of other professionals, I soaked up and exchanged knowledge. Mrs. Carrington was right; I needed my own experience. For the next several years, I thrived and soon advanced to become assistant supervisor (and acting supervisor) of psychiatric nursing service for the hospital."

Bette also fell in love. "I met him in 1959 at a party following a football game at Kenan Stadium. He was a graduate of UNC and UNC Law School. He practiced law with his father in a nearby town. As 1960 rolled around, we became engaged."

Winnie remained in Chapel Hill from 1955 through 1956, working on the psychiatric unit at North Carolina Memorial Hospital while her husband finished his last year of study. "We married the twenty-eighth day of August, 1955, and in the summer, we traveled to Interlochen, Michigan, to the National Music Camp, where I worked as a camp nurse. My husband and I continued our camp employment each summer until after our second child was born in 1961."

The fall of 1956 brought Winnie and her husband to Sampson County, North Carolina, where she worked as a staff nurse in a small hundred-bed hospital that was built with funding from the 1946 Hill Burton Act. This act provided federal assistance to states for building hospitals and health centers. "The hospital had no interns or residents, no staffed ER, and no recovery room—only stock bottles of medications, syringes and needles to be sterilized, orders to be taken (no ward secretaries), and patients to be cared for," she says.

During the day, most units were staffed with three registered nurses, two aides, and a floating orderly. The only two IV medications available were Terramycin and sulfadiazine. At North Carolina Memorial Hospital, nurses were not allowed to start IVs, but Winnie quickly learned this procedure, despite the fact that at that time there were no butterflies or IV catheters—only needles, tubing, and glass bottles filled with IV solutions.

Winnie later became head nurse on a combined surgical and pediatric unit, which meant rotating to the newly established recovery room when needed. Every other weekend, in the evenings, she was in charge of the emergency room—which was covered by only the head nurse and the floating orderly—and also acted as house supervisor. Since no physicians were in the hospital, individual physicians were called in for each patient. The head nurse also retrieved the supplies and medicines needed by each floor.

In 1959, Winnie and her husband moved into a house next to the surgical clinic in New Bern, North Carolina. "I became acquainted with the only two local surgeons due to my son having pyloric stenosis," Winnie recalls. "At that time, there was no anesthesiologist in New Bern, only a nurse anesthetist. The pediatric area of the one hospital in New Bern had no daytime registered-nurse coverage, so I naturally did this shift to care for him."

After a short period of time, Winnie began to fill in for the nurses at the surgical clinic and then worked part time for five years. "I learned many things, from taking X-rays to assisting with cast application and removal," she recalls. "We did tendon repairs, breast biopsies, sigmoidoscopies, wound suturing, and lesion removal. Many patients that came to the hospital's emergency room were sent to the surgical clinic."

After graduation, Pat worked in the psychiatric unit of the North Carolina Memorial Hospital for several months. The following June she joined the faculty of the UNC School of Nursing as an instructor in the OB-GYN and medical-surgical nursing classes, continuing in this position for four years. "In 1960, I moved to Goldsboro, North Carolina, and for the next ten years stayed at home raising my sons and participating in community activities."

At graduation, Martha was already married to Robert S. Cline, a medical student at UNC. She spent the next two years working in the operating rooms at North Carolina Memorial Hospital while he finished his medical degree.

"I rotated through general surgery as well as many of the specialty surgical services, such as chest surgery, neurosurgery, orthopedic surgery, urologic surgery, and reconstructive and plastic surgery," recalls Martha. During this time she observed the emergence of grafts (skin, vascular, bone, and others), and she also remembers that computers, radiology, and other technology were evolving and being introduced into the operating room.

In 1957, after her husband graduated from medical school, Martha and Bob moved to Charleston, South Carolina, where he was an intern. Martha stayed home and had their first child, Dara. After his internship was complete, they moved to New Orleans for two years so that Robert could fulfill his military obligation in the US Public Health Service. Their second child, Phillip, was born there. Martha was a stay-at-home mother, taking care of the two children. They then moved back to Charleston, where her husband completed a residency in internal medicine. In Charleston Martha represented the youth program called Y-teens for the YMCA.

Joy's first RN position was as a camp nurse at Camp Mondamin during the summer of 1955. This boys' camp was located in Tuxedo,

North Carolina. After that, she worked as a Public Health Nurse II at the Mecklenburg County Public Health Department in Charlotte until 1957. "This was an enjoyable experience, similar to our public health assignment in our senior year of nursing school," Joy recalls.

Within a short time, she married and had two daughters, Cathryne and Martha. During the summers from 1966 to 1973, she was the camp nurse at Camp Ton-A-Wandah. This girls' camp is nestled in the Blue Ridge Mountains of North Carolina in an area filled with lush green foliage, natural lakes, and waterfalls. The name Ton-A-Wandah means "by the fall of water." "I shared my own experiences with the girl campers, two of whom were my daughters, passing on my legacy," she recalls.

Joy as a bridesmaid in Geri's June 1955 wedding.

While raising her family, Joy remained active in hospital services as chairman of the Charlotte Memorial Hospital Auxiliary's Service Committee, coordinating activities of the Pink Ladies with those of the volunteers' service in the hospital. The Pink Ladies directed other volunteers and met with the hospital's board to discuss coordinating activities of the volunteers. Her position touched many depart-

Joy (center) as a camp nurse.

ments and services, including the book cart, library, flower desk, ER, outpatient departments, pediatrics, the mailroom, and other special services for patients. "My two little girls, ages five and ten, volunteered their wise guidance on shopping tours I made for toys for the pediatrics wing and goodies for the clinics. These were happy hours for me around the hospital, serving and leading others for patients' comfort," Joy says.

When she volunteered, Joy says that she tried to be near the emergency room, "where the action was," and she could learn about new medical treatments and refresh herself about old ones. This prepared her to return to nursing later in life.

Following graduation, Gloria moved to Windsor, North Carolina, where her husband, Don, had a temporary job measuring land. She began working primarily evenings and nights at the Windsor Hospital. This small hospital had less than 120 beds and was segregated, with white patients on the third floor and "colored" patients on second floor.

"I often worked on the second floor, finding I was the only white person on the floor," Gloria recalls. "This position was quite a challenge compared to nursing school. I had to learn how to begin an IV, but other than that, it was just practicing what we had learned."

One night while Gloria was on the "colored floor," a patient went into labor with her sixth child. "We knew this would be a quick delivery, and soon we were holding a newborn," Gloria recalls. "I told the other nurse that the patient still looked large. I listened to her uterus with a fetoscope and heard another heartbeat. I went out to the desk and called the doctor. It was about 4:00 a.m., and he said, 'well, you did all right with the first one; you will do fine with the other. I will see you in the morning.' We delivered the second baby and placenta, cleaned up our patient, and I took her back to her room. That was an exciting night."

Gloria worked in Windsor for five months until Don left for basic training in San Antonio, Texas.

Sally's first job was as a night nurse in Gravely Sanatorium in Chapel Hill. Just two days after graduation she began working the midnight to 8:00 a.m. shift, with ten days on and four days off. "I learned new nursing procedures, including how to conduct gastric washings," Sally recalls. "I was also responsible for nursing care of patients with tuberculosis."

She worked at Gravely Sanatorium until Labor Day of 1955, when she moved to Atlanta and began employment as a private duty nurse with the Georgia Nursing Association. She cared for postsurgical patients as a private duty nurse. For the most part, her patients were at Georgia Baptist Hospital, but she sometimes worked at Emory University Hospital as well.

"At that time almost every surgical patient employed private duty nurses for a least the first two postsurgical days. This was more complicated at Emory, where I took care of patients who had had chest surgery. Private duty involved learning the rules, regulations, and facilities that were unique to each hospital."

In November, 1955, she stopped work as a private duty nurse and began working for the DeKalb County Health Department. "In the initial interview, the nursing director inquired about my marriage plans and contraception," she recalls. At that time, it was permissible and routine practice for an employer to ask about plans for marriage and children.

Her first assignment was the main center in Decatur, Georgia, and she later moved to the Doraville office. In both offices, she had a geographic area for which she was responsible for patients with cardiac conditions, pregnant women, and children.

"When the Grady Hospital Clinic prescribed antibiotics to children, I went into their homes and administered injections on Monday through Friday. They were supposed to go back to Grady for medications on the weekend, but rarely did. I carried an extra syringe and an ampoule of adrenalin to be used in case of an adverse reaction, but, fortunately, I never had to use it. The backup physician was miles away."

Sally also ran the Well Child Clinic (WCC) and Maternity Clinic. "When not around patients, we called the WCC the Wild Child Clinic," she says. "We knew that if the first child receiving an immunization cried, we would have a long day of crying children."

Sally married John Nicholson on January 22, 1956. In 1958, she had a miscarriage while they were in North Carolina for Christmas. On the way home, John, who had Marfan's Syndrome, began to have cardiac difficulties. In 1959, he died of an aneurysm in Atlanta, where they were living.

Sally then entertained the idea of becoming a medical missionary with the Mission Board of the United Church of Christ, going as far as getting a project assignment. The Mission Board wanted her to start a diploma school of nursing in Turkey, but she told the board that she really had no idea what starting a diploma school of nursing would involve. The board responded by telling her, "You know more than anyone there." Sally's response was, "Then you are in real trouble." Her pastor also advised against this move because it would not be a good place to meet another potential husband.

Sally decided to pursue a master's degree at Emory University. She transferred from the clinics at Grady to the DeKalb County Health Department in Atlanta, where she remained until she began at Emory in 1960 on a scholarship.

After graduation, Louise was married and then shortly later took the state boards. "Thanks to Mrs. Alice Gifford, community health was the field of nursing that really caught my interest, and the experience in public health nursing at Cabarrus County Health Department was the clincher for me," says Louise.

After a brief stint on the medical floor at North Carolina Memorial Hospital, she was ready to pursue her public health nursing career. "My first employment was as a generalized public health nurse in a large county," she says. "I was assigned to a specific area of the county that included five schools and an already established family caseload.

In addition to my district nursing visits, I helped in clinics held at the health department as well as in small surrounding towns."

In 1958, Louise put her nursing career on hold to raise her children. However, in 1976, the opportunity to return to public health nursing came knocking at her door. "For the next twenty years, I worked in a small health department as a public health nurse supervisor," she says. "Needless to say, by 1976, much had changed in the delivery of public health services in North Carolina. State health services were now regionalized, and there were wonderful nurse consultants for every facet of public health nursing. Although the basic concepts of public health nursing remained, the delivery of these services was changing due to federal and state funding for health care."

During her time in public health nursing, Louise took part in the "swine flu" immunization program that was in effect from 1976 to 1977. This program was halted when some recipients died and cases of Guillain-Barré syndrome were found among persons receiving swine flu immunizations.

Louise saw the clinical services available in the health department expand, including a growing family-planning and maternity program with a nurse practitioner. The health department also began to provide health screenings, in house and in the community, for children and adults. Louise also witnessed the development of a constantly updated immunization program to reduce childhood communicable diseases, the implementation of new drugs and a regimen to control and reduce incidents

Louise in the early 1980s.

of tuberculosis, and the HIV/AIDs epidemic with all the associated issues it presented. "The electronic age was just around the corner, when it was time for me to retire," she says.

Although the Korean War had ended in 1953, the draft remained in place to ensure there was adequate manpower for occupying forces in Germany and Japan after World War II and the Korean War, the escalating Cold War, and the emerging conflict in Vietnam. The draft also motivated many to volunteer for military service so that they could choose the branch of service in which to serve. There was a separate draft for physicians during this time. With so many men training for or serving in the military, several of the new School of Nursing graduates traveled with their husbands to faraway places.

On September 24, 1955, Rae married Ed Starnes, who was her college sweetheart and a UNC journalism major. He attended pilot training and then went to Greenville Air Force Base in Mississippi, where he received his wings. The couple then relocated to Tyndall Air Force Base in Florida for fighter training, which was followed by an assignment to Kirtland Air Force Base in New Mexico.

In New Mexico, Rae and Ed lived in Chama, a very small community near the Colorado border. "This isolated area was like living in another country," Rae remembers. "Ed caught trout in a stream behind our house and went bear hunting with another officer. Feeding deer would brush up against the house at night. Since Ed's duties sometimes required him to be away for several nights in a row, we bought a rifle and pistol, and I learned to shoot them."

The wife of a retired army colonel (who had survived the Bataan Death March) befriended Rae, and the few women in Chama included her in their bridge club—the only social activity in town. There was no hospital nearby, so when Rae became pregnant, she had to travel thirty miles to reach the only doctor in the area for prenatal checkups. On delivery day they drove to a hospital in Los Alamos, almost seventy-five miles away.

"After a wild ride through the mountains (including two flat tires, a transfer to a pickup truck, and then to a station wagon) our first child, Ed III, was born on September 19, 1956," Rae recalls. "When I awakened from the anesthesia, a nurse with a beatific face and name-plate, 'Mrs. Jesus,' was bending over me. Heavenly music filled the air. I thought I had died. The music was a tradition at the Baptist Missionary Hospital, and I soon realized that Jesus wasn't married, so I didn't have to worry about Ed raising our child alone."

Following his tour of duty, they moved to Ed's hometown, Arlington, Virginia. He accepted a management-training position with Home Life Insurance Company in January, 1958. "We loved the cultural advantages of the DC area—art museums, history on every corner, and music concerts," Rae says.

Rae and Ed's second child, Kathryn Ramelle, was born on September 27, 1960. With the creation of NASA and the Marshall Space Flight Center in Huntsville, Alabama, Ed's company needed someone to open an office there to accommodate obligations to NASA. "It was a great opportunity to return to the South, and in 1961 Huntsville became our permanent home. Our sons Bill and David were born here in 1964 and 1968. Three of our four adult children and their families live in Huntsville."

Geri's first professional position was in pediatrics at the hospital in Glen Ridge, New Jersey (where her husband was born in 1933). She then joined her husband, Bob, for his tour of duty in the air force—first at Sampson Air Force Base in Geneva, New York (now closed), where she was a civilian nurse at the base hospital, then in San Antonio, Texas, where she was a pediatric nurse at Santa Rosa Hospital.

"Our next step was the American Institute for Foreign Trade in Glendale, Arizona," she recalls. "I took some classes in area studies and language. We studied Portuguese, hoping to go to Brazil, and I worked part time at St. Joseph's Hospital in Phoenix."

After Bob finished graduate school, Chase Manhattan Bank hired him in its International Division in New York City. His first international position was in San Juan, Puerto Rico, where their baby girl, Elicia, was born. "She was the only long, skinny, reddish-blond baby with no hair," Geri remembers. "All the other babies were chubby with lots of dark black hair."

After a couple of years, Chase transferred them to Buenos Aires, and so they learned Spanish. "I did not work professionally, but I was getting my international travel even without being an airline stewardess and also learning about medical treatment in other countries and cultures."

In 1963, Bob was called back to Chase Manhattan Bank head office in New York City, where they settled down for many years, except for two years that they spent in London in the late 1970s.

"I finally had an opportunity to catch up in my own career," Geri says. "First I was an instructor in the School of Nursing at Long Island College Hospital in Brooklyn and then an instructor in the Manpower Development Training Program of New York City."

With her university diploma and nursing license in hand, Janet was ready to assume an entirely new life in her dual role of wife and nurse. She moved to Champaign, Illinois, to join Bill, who was stationed at nearby Chanute Air Base. They decided to live in Champaign, home of the University of Illinois, because of its similarities to Chapel Hill.

"We lived in a rambling, older, large house that was remodeled into separate furnished apartments for married students," Janet recalls. "I was just so happy to be there with Bill that I hardly noticed the sparse furnishings, including the worn sofa that sagged somewhat in the middle. We had an enclosed, screened porch with little heat or air conditioning. It was so cold during the winter that we moved the mattress into the 'living room' to keep warm. This Southern girl never really adjusted to the bitter-cold weather."

Janet began interviewing with several medical facilities, looking for a position with regular hours and no shift changes. Eventually she chose the multispecialty Christie Clinic, which was very well known in the area for quality care and had the same pay scale as the hospital. "They were eager to hire me and had an immediate opening in the Ophthalmology Department," Janet remembers. "The department included three doctors as well as an older physician, Dr. Edward Albers, who had practiced for several years at the Mayo Clinic and was heralded as a brilliant physician."

Dr. Albers was on vacation during Janet's first week of work, and she was often asked if she would still be at the clinic when he returned. "He had quite the reputation for frequent nurse changes, but we had been taught to proceed in any situation, so my standard reply was always, 'Of course!'"

The following week, Janet noticed a man walking down the hall toward the Ophthalmology Department. He was very tall, large in stature, and muscular, and he wore thick shoes and heavy glasses. As he proceeded to Dr. Albers's office, he said quite gruffly, "Good morning," to which Janet responded with a cheerful greeting.

So here he was—Janet's first boss. Shortly, his buzzer rang number one, the signal to come to his office. As she entered, he immediately asked, "Who are you?" Janet explained that she was the new nurse. The next question, "Where are you from?" was frequently asked of Janet because of her Southern dialect. She told him about Chapel Hill, the new nursing school at UNC, and the reason she was in Illinois. He actually smiled, congratulated her on her degree, and seemed happy that she could join his staff. Then Dr. Albers sternly said, "I tell you something *one* time and *one* time only, and that is my philosophy," to which Janet replied simply, "Yes, sir."

"I listened carefully, and consequently, I required no repetition of orders," she recalls. "Our training at UNC was similar, as we were expected to remember what we learned by *listening*. This, to me, was the most important lesson then, and in the years to come."

Janet and Dr. Albers worked well together. "I enjoyed the experience, and gained valuable knowledge about the anatomy and physiology of the eye," she says. "Cataract surgery was quite major at that time, and transplants were in their infancy. I recall transporting an eye for an emergency situation while Dr. Albers waited in the surgical area. I was instructed to drive *very* slowly to the hospital to keep the movement of the container to a minimum. The surgery was a success, thank goodness."

After two years there, a nurse replaced Janet for a semester while she and Bill returned to Chapel Hill so that Bill could complete a semester of courses he needed for air force educational status. "Dean Kemble heard this news and offered me an assistant instructor position at the School of Nursing," Janet recalls. "I was elated to return to a scene so familiar. My assignment was to instruct and supervise students in the Outpatient Department and Gravely Center rotation. I enjoyed every minute of this wonderful, challenging, and rewarding opportunity. My biggest regret in life is not continuing this course of action in my career."

After the semester ended, they returned to Illinois, and Janet went back to work at the clinic. "The next year, I became pregnant, and Bill was shipped to Japan for an emergency assignment in the air force. I moved back home to Chapel Hill, where in July, I delivered a healthy baby girl, Jana Lee. In November, Bill was discharged and returned home from Japan to welcome his new daughter. We were a little family now."

Janet's dad offered Bill the chance to join him in the family restaurant business, The Pines Restaurant. This was an opportunity for

Bill to learn the operational, administration, and management side of the restaurant profession. Soon afterward, a second restaurant, The College Inn, was opened in Raleigh near the North Carolina State University campus. "Together, we assumed responsibility for this establishment, and I assisted with training, supervising and bookkeeping, among other duties," Janet says. "This still gave me time to be with Jana, now six years old, and to stay involved in her many activities. After a few years, The College Inn was sold to the university for athletes' housing." Coincidentally, Janet's grandson who was captain of the North Carolina State University soccer team would many years later reside there. After the sale of The College Inn, Janet and Bill moved back to Chapel Hill to resume working with her parents, who were aging and needed assistance.

"During these years, while I was out of my nursing career, I kept my license active and occasionally worked on a temporary basis in doctors' offices," Janet says. "This enabled me to keep up my nursing skills and to stay abreast of updates and changes in the profession."

In January of 1956, Gloria and Don traveled to Sheppard Air Force Base in Wichita Falls, Texas, where Don began auditing school, and she began work at Sheppard Air Force Hospital.

Gloria was delighted to be assigned to the maternity ward. "However, when I reported for work, my assignment was changed to the crash ward along with an officers' ward and an airmen's ward," she recalls. "I nearly flipped, as I felt inadequate for the crash ward. The six months I was there proved very valuable. We received burn, accident, and critical-care patients. The crash ward had about twenty beds with just curtains for dividers."

Gloria remembers one patient who was brought in and placed right beside the nurse's station. She had had an appendectomy and neglected to tell the doctor she was asthmatic. While under anesthesia, she had an attack and was left in a coma. "This was so heartbreaking, as she was about my age."

Gloria left Wichita Falls in early June, and Don left for Japan at the end of June. Gloria stayed with her parents until August, when she flew to Tokyo to join Don at Tachikawa Air Force Base. "For the six weeks I was with my parents, I worked at the local Thomasville Hospital. I hardly adjusted before it was time to leave. They were very good to me."

"Life during our service years in Japan was great," Gloria says. "Our first child (daughter) was born in December after I arrived in August. For about a year, I volunteered in the maternity clinic on Fridays. The hospital did not hire civilians. I also became involved with the Red Cross and became the director for the base for about two years. Our second child (son) was born in October of 1958 and was only eight weeks old when we returned to the states."

While they were in Tachikawa, Janet's husband, Bill, came to the base. He was enlisted and not supposed to leave his quarters. Don talked with the officers in charge, who arranged for Bill to come to their house one evening. "What a wonderful treat for the three of us," Gloria says. "Another visit was from my high school Latin teacher. These visits were highlights of our time away from home. No one traveled like they do today. We only called home three or four times, as it was so expensive. How wonderful it would have been to have cell phones."

Just ten days after taking the state boards in Raleigh, Donna boarded the train in Winston-Salem, North Carolina. It was bound for Central Station in New York City, where Donna joined other dependents on a military flight to Europe. Donna's husband, Brantley, was a first lieutenant flying C-119s in a troop carrier squadron stationed at Neubiberg Air Base near Munich, Germany.

After meeting Brantley in Germany, Donna experienced her first high-speed run on a German autobahn in Brantley's 1951 black Plymouth. "We took scenic detours, and I shall never forget the devastation of Mainz," she recalls.

Mainz was the industrial center and economic lifeline for the western part of the German war machine and thus a major target for Allied bombing during the war. "Less than a decade after the war, driving through the city along the river was startling. Tall buildings were gutted. All the front walls were completely sheared off, and you could see the various apartment rooms with their blue, pink, yellow, or green walls and, occasionally, even a fixture or a piece of furniture still in the room. No one was even walking on the streets, and we were stunned into silence because we could not believe what we were seeing."

Donna and Brantley lived in Europe for three years. In Munich, Donna went to Neubiberg Air Base with the hope of being a nurse at the clinic. "I was disappointed when they told me that they were only hiring Germans because of the Marshall Plan of putting Germans back to work and rebuilding their economy," Donna recalls.

Two months later, Donna found herself taking the Orient Express through Yugoslavia to Athens, where Brantley was sent for temporary duty. The day after she boarded the train, Donna learned that the seasonal Orient Express was no longer a through train because the tourist season had ended the week before. She would have to leave the train in Belgrade and board another local train to her destination. "I worried because my visa only allowed me to travel through the country, not to get off the train," recalls Donna. When she arrived in Belgrade, she left the train without any problem and spent the night there.

Donna at the Acropolis in Athens, 1955.

After a long trip from Belgrade, the train arrived in Athens. However, no one was there to meet her. "I knew Brantley was in Athens, but I did not have an address. The only thing I could think of was that American Express could find another American if anyone could. I had just turned to leave the platform in search of an American Express when I heard long running steps getting closer. I turned around, and there was Brantley, out of breath."

For two days Brantley had met all incoming trains and had even spoken with the chaplain at the US Embassy. He had made so many trips to the train station that his motorcycle ran out of gas on the day Donna arrived.

In Athens, Brantley rented a house from a sea captain's wife that was totally floored with white marble. She, her son, and their maid had moved into the basement to earn some extra spending money while her husband was at sea. "The house was near the top of a hill, and in the morning planes taking off from the nearby airport had little time to gain altitude as they roared over the house and startled us out of bed," Donna recalls. "I remember going straight for the cold marble floor one morning."

Life was a new adventure as Donna washed uniforms in the bathtub and ironed them on the kitchen table. Chunks of ice were delivered to keep the refrigerator cool, and in the morning the turkey salesman herded a large flock of big black-and-white-feathered, gobbling turkeys with a very long and limber stick, continually corralling them back on the road.

The motorcycle gave them freedom to explore Athens and its surroundings. "We saw wonderful things along the coast, even watching some ongoing archeological digs. One day we drove up to the steps of the Acropolis, and no one else was there."

After this great assignment ended, they headed back to Munich—Donna by train and Brantley via plane. A day and a half later, Brantley was in Munich, waiting again for Donna's train to arrive. This time a washed-out bridge in Croatia brought the delay, and the passengers had to take buses across the mountain road to a place with just a few houses, one of which was the train station. "Some hours later we heard an encouraging sound of a train whistle coming from the opposite direction," Donna says.

Donna clearly remembers her elation as the train pulled into the glass-covered tracks of the Munich Hauptbahnhof. "I was home! Oktoberfest was coming soon, and I knew that the next summer (1956) we would have our first child, Martha. Happily, my nursing career would begin at home."

Within the next year, the entire Forty-First Squadron was transferred to Evreux Air Base in France, farther away from the potential Cold War battle line between East and West Germany. "We were sorry to leave Germany, but we packed up and drove to Paris with ten-month-old Martha sitting in her car seat between us," Donna recalls. "When we arrived in Paris, in the center of a myriad of avenues rose the majestic neoclassical Arc de Triomphe, which set the bar for all monuments. As we drove down the Avenue des Champs-Élysées, we marveled at all the trees with their delicate spring leaves and the outdoor cafes. It truly seemed like an April-in-Paris movie set."

They moved into a government housing area called La Madeleine in the village of Evreux, approximately sixty kilometers from Paris. "Summer and fall passed quickly, and the proverbial French unions, who often went on strike, did not disrupt our lives until winter, when the power grid would periodically shut down over a union grievance," Donna says.

"Our one-story duplex was on a concrete slab with heat coming in at the ceiling. Too often we did not have any electricity, and it was so cold that Martha slept in her snowsuit between us. We bought an Aladdin heater that burned kerosene, closely huddling around it and even frying eggs in a pan on top. I vividly remember trying to dry cloth diapers on the line. I'd put a clothespin in one corner, and by the time I was ready to pin the other, it had frozen with swag in it. All I could think of was that we'd have more diapers to dry in another six months, when our second child arrived."

After college, Virginia worked as a nurse and eventually met her husband in Pensacola. They were married in the late 1950s and traveled quite a bit, as her husband was in the navy.

Virginia's daughter, Kelly, recalls that her mom stayed home to raise her children and that Virginia loved to cook, play bridge, and garden while they were young. As her children grew older, Virginia took up bowling and tennis and became an avid reader and sports fan—especially of the Redskins and Tar Heels. She developed fairly severe arthritis in her fifties, but still enjoyed her friends and bridge and garden clubs.

"She had some rough final years, but excluding them, I think you could best describe her as a happy person who loved her family and friends and enjoyed her life," Kelly says. "She was always proud to be a nurse, keeping her license up to date and reading all the latest journals. Mom had a lot of friends and always went out of her way to be helpful to them."

Virginia Edwards Coupe died on January 9, 1995.

While working in the North Carolina Memorial Hospital in early May, 1960, Bette became acutely ill. "For almost a week I could not move any part of myself without great pain, extreme weakness, and fatigue," Bette remembers. "I was so exhausted that it was difficult to lift or use my arms. I could not shake the thermometer down to check a low-grade fever. It felt like a severe case of the flu with migratory arthralgia."

Numerous comprehensive lab tests proved negative without leading to a definitive diagnosis, and the doctors concluded that Bette had a viral infection. After a month at home, Bette's acute symptoms gradually receded enough for her to try working again.

"I had never been sick like this and felt guilty about not working," she recalls. "During the summer months I kept working, becoming easily fatigued despite the minimal physical exertion required in my job as the psychiatric assistant supervisor in nursing. Slowly I began to regain some strength and feel a little better. Regardless, I was happy to be making some progress and planning the future with my fiancé."

By November, it was evident that Bette's illness had not run its course, when she relapsed with a return of debilitating muscle fatigue. This time another nurse shared similar symptoms. Dr. T. Franklin Williams, a remarkable Harvard graduate on the staff of North Carolina Memorial Hospital, became their physician and remained so for the next few years. After tests and consultations with the Centers for Disease Control, he concluded that they had myalgic encephalomyelitis (ME).

"At last it had a name. However, at that time, not much was known about the course or outcome of ME, which turned out to be lengthy and unpredictable," Bette says. "Later, ME would be well documented as a syndrome that typically follows a viral infection, which may be subclinical, in previously fit and active young adults, mostly women."

Not able to work, Bette's only choice was to live with her parents in Augusta, Georgia. "I shall be forever grateful they were willing and able to care for me. None of us knew when I would recover my health, so I broke my engagement."

Over the next three difficult years, Bette gradually recovered enough to start working full time in nursing in the fall of 1964, when Bette began as a staff nurse on a busy medical unit at the VA Hospital in Dallas. "Every day, I collapsed when I got home, but I didn't have any relapses."

Six months later she accepted a position as head nurse on another medical unit. "All the team nursing I had learned in classes and clinical areas as a student came back to me," Bette says. "In the beginning, I was the new kid on the block. Organizing and delivering patient-centered care to forty patients was challenging and humbling, especially since the head nurse supposedly possesses clinical expertise."

Bette learned from working with patients and staff, eventually giving back to them, too. Most of the time she was one of two RNs on the day shift, which meant she was in charge of the unit and also a team leader for some patients. "My five years as a head nurse led me to believe that this role is the most important and rewarding nursing role in a hospital," she says.

Bette had spent several years focused on becoming healthy and fully functional again, with the hope to work in nursing if possible. "Now that I had recovered without residual effects, I began thinking seriously about my future career. I loved being a head nurse but did not want to do this for the rest of my life," she recalled. "The head nurse role opened my thoughts to developing the leadership role of clinical nurses, and my interest was additionally stimulated by an article published in 1958 that

Bette makes notes for a nursing in-service education program at the VA Hospital in Dallas.

looked at the nurse's contribution in the doctor-nurse-patient social system."[7]

Bette was aware that the psychological needs of many medical-surgical patients were not being met because the needs were either not recognized or were misunderstood. "With all the demands on a nurse, there was little time to concentrate on this aspect of care. I began thinking how I might integrate this dimension. I had a good background in medical and psychiatric nursing and wanted to further develop an awareness of the social-psychological components of care essential in nursing. So, I chose to pursue a master's degree in psychiatric nursing and become a clinical nurse specialist. Dr. David S. Fuller, a friend on the faculty at the University of Texas Southwestern Medical School and consultation-liaison psychiatrist for the Dallas VA Medical Center, was influential in my vision for a similar role in nursing."

Around this time, Bette's UNC classmates and friends Donna and Sally were encouraging her to join the US Air Force Reserve (USAFR). Donna's husband, Brantley, was a pilot in the USAFR, and Sally was a flight nurse. "Early in 1969, Brantley swore me in as a captain in the USAFR in their living room. The monthly weekend drill money would come in handy in graduate school, and nurses were needed in the height of the Vietnam War." Bette remained with the USAFR until retiring in 1989.

After spending a year teaching at the UNC Chapel Hill School of Nursing, Sara sold her typewriter, toured a few European countries, and then went to work in Frankfurt, Germany. Her uncle was in charge of the occupation forces at that time and was able to get Sara a position in the US Army Ninety-Seventh General Hospital.

From 1956 to 1957, she worked in the intensive care, recovery, and emergency units at the US Army Ninety-Seventh General Hospital in Frankfurt, Germany. Donna remembers that Sara came to Munich to visit her and Brantley. "What a treat it was to see Sara get off the train at the Hauptbahnhof, wearing the latest fashion trend: red tennis shoes and American blue jeans. 'Amihose,' as they were called in German slang, were the most desirable clothing item for the young people at that time."

After Germany, Sara worked in New York City for a year or so, primarily for a bank. She also worked part time at Doctors Hospital, where she cared for Judy Garland as a patient. Sara and two friends then applied to work for the Arabian American Oil Company (ARAMCO) in Saudi Arabia. They were accepted, and Sara became a district head nurse.

ARAMCO provided health-care services for its employees and their dependents through a large central health center in Dhahran and smaller primary-care health centers in outlying districts. Sara provided nursing supervision for a district primary health center in Ras Tamura, a seaport north of Dhahran, Saudi Arabia. This facility included thirty-two patient beds, an emergency room, and facilities for labor and delivery. The center processed approximately 120,000 outpatient visits annually.

In 1961, Sara met her future husband, Don. In 1960, he had started working in health administration for ARAMCO and had met Sara during a January business trip to the satellite hospital where she worked. They became engaged the very next month. In March, Sara flew back to the United States and was met at the airport by Don's father and mother, who lived in New Jersey. It was Don's father who presented Sara with her engagement ring. In May, Sara and her mother spent a month touring Europe. They met the rest of the wedding party in Rome, where they were married in the Church of Santa Susanna.

They lived in Dhahran after they married. Sara was no longer an employee of the oil company but worked there under a different status as Don's wife. In addition to developing, supervising, and teaching staff-training programs at the primary health center, she developed and implemented maternal and child health, tuberculosis, and nutritional programs.

Sara and Don on their wedding day.

Sara and the other nurses worked intimately with the Bedouin women and children. The Bedouin are a predominantly desert-dwelling Arabian ethnic group. "We started with the basics. During one of the first classes, surrounded by several mothers and their children, I demonstrated how to bathe a baby, being sure to take special care for the eyes (there was a high incidence of trachoma)," recalls Sara. "The next week when the class convened again, the same baby was brought back to have his bath. I explained to the mother that the previous demonstration was meant to teach her how to do it. She looked at me as if I were out of my mind, and then explained that she had to walk five miles to the well and carry water back to her home. She was not about to use that precious water to bathe a child. Besides, she said, I did a better job."

When Sara first arrived, the local midwives were delivering babies in the villages. "One of their customs was to pack the vagina with salt following the delivery, which led to difficulty for the next pregnancy and delivery. At first, it was difficult to persuade the women to come to the clinic, but through the prenatal and postnatal program that we developed, we saw a real difference in just three years."

"My experience in Saudi Arabia was very rewarding, allowing me to implement nursing principles instilled in me by my UNC education," Sara says. "It was exciting to be involved in developing an integrated preventive and curative medical-care program."

During the 1960s, Sara concentrated most of her energies on rearing her family, but she also worked part time in the central Dhahran Outpatient Department, which had approximately 220,000 visits annually.

Sara, her husband, and their three children lived in Dhahran Camp, a residential community ARAMCO built for its employees. In June, 1967, during the Six Day War, Israeli forces took control of the Gaza Strip and Sinai Peninsula from Egypt, Golan Heights from Syria, and the West Bank and East Jerusalem from Jordan. Early one morning during the Six Day War, the Dhahran camp gates were closed, and families were instructed to remain in their homes as rumors of anti-American uprisings circulated in the camp.

A ten-foot cement wall surrounding Sara's house provided traditional Arabian privacy for a well-tended garden. In the front and back were large wooden gates with seldom-used weighty bolts and a small window for viewing callers. The ringing of strings of camel bells attached to both gates announced visitors.

"I put Sharon and Mike to bed for an afternoon nap," Sara says. "From their bedroom, through multiple paned windows, I could see the front garden and gate. Linda, only eighteen months old, lay sleeping in her crib in a back bedroom. I wandered into the kitchen."

Sara's friend Sheila from Abqaiq called to see if Sara knew what was happening. Sara told her what she had heard: that a crowd had gotten through the front gates and marched to the administration building. Sara could hear the noise of the mob but could not see anything from her house, where all the doors and gates were locked. While they were on the phone, Sara suddenly realized that people were coming over their wall.

"Howling Arab youths were scaling the wall, and the sound of breaking glass told me they were hurling stones at the front windows," Sara says. "I raced down the hall to rescue Sharon and Mike. The drawn blinds prevented the shattering glass from reaching across the room to the bunk beds of the two sleeping children. Quickly pulling them from their warm beds, I deposited both in the middle of our king-sized bed in the back bedroom, told them to stay put, and sped to check on Linda, still sleeping peacefully in her crib."

Sara's first act was to scurry to the kitchen, grab a box of cookies, a carton of milk, and some glasses, then race back to the bedroom. The mob had several bolted doors to batter in before they could reach her. Linda, sleeping soundly, was completely unaware of the turmoil. Sharon and Mike were happily occupied having a picnic in the middle of Mom and Dad's bed, which would be forbidden at other times. Sara sat in front of the dressing table, let down her long hair, and proceeded to try a new upsweep style. "Perhaps I felt I had to act normal so the children would not know how truly frightened I was," she recalls. "It was not a conscious act."

Suddenly, the sounds of angry voices diminished, and it was clear that the crowd had moved out into the street. Another group surged into the alley behind their house and began attacking cars and buildings there. "I later learned an Arab neighbor came to our rescue by shouting, 'No Americans there!' Don called several times from the hospital. A sea of angry people separated us, and there was no possible way for him to reach the house. We were safe, I assured him."

The Saudi government was embarrassed over the incident and immediately put tighter security around the camp, but three days later ARAMCO decided to offer voluntary evacuation to American families anyway. Unbeknownst to Sara, Don helped the company make the decision that the first departing plane should carry all pregnant women, mothers, and young children. Sara was five months pregnant with her daughter Donna.

Sara wrote the following account of her family's evacuation from Saudi Arabia:

> Evacuation was to be much more stressful than remaining in Dhahran. Due to the unrest, scheduled flights to Saudi Arabia had been canceled. When ARAMCO appealed for help, an airline crew, on stopover time in Athens, volunteered to make the flight.
>
> At the airport, a plane waited on the runway, fueled and ready to depart, but it did not have government clearance for takeoff. For five hours, we sat on the floor of the non-air-conditioned building with two hundred other women and children.
>
> Finally, we received permission to leave. I shall always remember the reception the crew gave us. They worked calmly and efficiently, with bright smiles and good humor, to organize a completely chaotic scene. The plane was stocked with games, diapers, milk, juices, baby food, and real American cookies.
>
> Five minutes after we left the ground, the captain's voice came over the speaker. "Ladies, I just received a report that I think will be of interest to you. The war is over!" There was dead silence for a few seconds, followed by uncontrollable laughter.
>
> We could not return to Saudi Arabia. Even the captain did not know where we were going. He kept us informed each time he received a different directive. An hour before we were due to land in Athens, he received

a directive to fly on to Rome. During the flight, Mike became quieter and quieter. I soon realized he was ill and feverish.

We landed safely in Rome and went by bus directly to a summer resort, opened early to accommodate us. We were deposited in the lobby awaiting assignment of rooms. Because Mike was so sick, they tried to get us out of the lobby as quickly as possible, but we were put in a tiny room, with only one bed, not even a full-sized one, to sleep the four of us. At this point, I broke down and cried hysterically. It was not what the children needed, but it certainly moved some Italian authorities. We were soon changed to a larger room, arriving there at the same time as an Italian doctor. By then, Mike had a 105-degree temperature. The doctor gave him an injection of penicillin, wrote out some prescriptions, and left, and I began to frantically apply cold wet towels and try to get fluids down him.

To add to the problems, our luggage was lost en route. I was out of diapers and lacked a change of clothes for the children. The situation became critical. The manager of the hotel appeared, with a maid carrying a tray loaded with cereal, eggs, bread, butter, jam, fresh fruit, and juices. We were starved. What a banquet it was for us.

The manager also took the prescriptions and sent someone into the village to wake the local pharmacist. At midnight, the medications arrived at our door along with a fresh supply of diapers. Around five o'clock in the morning, Mike's fever finally broke. As he was sleeping peacefully, I crawled into bed beside him, falling asleep myself.

As we were leaving Saudi Arabia, I had teamed up with an English friend and her four children. Our husbands worked together, and John had asked me to stay with Eileen. They had three older boys and a girl about the same age as Mike. The boys were so upset over the unsettling events, they resorted to screaming at each other and their mother, and even physical fighting. Eileen simply could not handle them. She had no place to go in the UK or in the States. I promised her that no matter where we went, we would stay together.

We decided to try to get an apartment in Rome, settle down there, and wait for permission from the embassy to return to Arabia. All visas to travel to the Mideast had been canceled. Then a call came through from my mother in North Carolina. My father was in the hospital with a bleeding ulcer. I decided we should go there.

New York customs and immigration officials had witnessed evacuees returning home for several days. We must have presented a very dispirited picture as we stumbled through the gates. I had been carrying Linda, but I had to put her down while I collected the baggage. She wandered along following Sharon, who tightly clutched Mike's hand. Suddenly her white, frilly, plastic-lined panties dropped to her ankles. Her diaper was soaked, and the weight had been too much. Realizing her predicament, she modestly turned her back to the people at the customs counter and bent over to try to pull the panties up, revealing a lovely white bottom surrounded by a frilly petticoat.

A tall black customs official jumped over the counter, retrieved the sagging panties, scooped her up in his arms, and said, "Thank God, honey, you made it into the good ole United States before you lost your britches. Welcome home!" Putting her on his shoulders, he winked at me and said, "You can pick them up after you get your things sorted out." Taking Mike and Sharon with him, he placed them all on the counter, where they were the center of attention of several laughing customs officials. It was good to be home!

The flight to New Bern was uneventful. My father was to be hospitalized for two more weeks, so we moved in with my mom. Three weeks passed before Don could contact us by telephone. We were unable to get much news of what was happening in Dhahran. I was on the phone every day talking to the American embassy in Washington. They assured me that all was quiet in the ARAMCO camp and that we could soon get our visas to return. Hearing Don's voice and knowing that he was all right were such a relief. He talked to all the children. I could see them relax and begin to believe that everything was going to turn out right after all. Sharon's nightmares ceased.

I continued to hound the embassy in Washington. I was determined to give birth to our fourth child in Saudi Arabia with my husband. Time was running out. In August we received our visas. We flew from New York to London with the Wernsdorfers. It was a rough flight, and we arrived at Heathrow with seven airsick children.

We separated from the Wernsdorfers in London. They flew on to Dhahran. We flew to Milan, where Don arranged to meet us. He was waiting at the gate when we arrived, and Sharon, spying her father, went flying past all the customs and immigration officials straight into her father's arms. Mike and Linda toddled behind, big smiles on their faces. Our family was complete again.

---

[7] M. A. Johnson and H. W. Martin (1958). A Sociological Analysis of the Nurse Role. *Am J Nursing* 58:373-377.

Bette used this paper in writing her essay for graduate school. One of the authors, Dr. Martin, worked for a number of years as the coordinator of the curriculum research project at the UNC Chapel Hill School of Nursing and later transferred to the Psychiatry Department at the University of Texas Southwestern Medical School in Dallas, where he was a research sociologist.

8

Early Gatherings and Reunions

Upon graduation, the class of 1955 became chartered members of the Alumni Association of the School of Nursing of UNC Chapel Hill, with Martha presiding as its first president. The association established a means of continuing the ties of friendship among the alumni, and nearly sixty years later, relationships, connections, and activities that began at UNC still flourish.

"At every turn, the School of Nursing Alumni Association was instrumental in promoting or assisting us in keeping a sense of place and purpose with our alma mater," says Bette, who was the student representative on the committee tasked with writing the constitution and bylaws that established the association.

In 1960, the first nursing class celebrated five years since graduation. In their honor, the School of Nursing Alumni Association sponsored a reunion dinner at The Carolina Inn. "It was a double treat to see each other and be recipients of our active alumni association," Bette says. "Five years since graduation, we delighted in seeing each other and catching up on news. It was a long, happy day."

In 1961, the class had raised enough money for a hand-painted oil portrait of Dean Kemble, and an unveiling ceremony was scheduled. As freshman president of the first class, Janet presented their gift to the dean, ten years after they had begun their journey at UNC.

Dean Kemble's portrait.

"The beautiful painting was unveiled with flourish, admiration, and applause," recalls Janet. "Even the dean had twinkling eyes and showed the warm smile we knew so well. The painting hangs at the School of Nursing where everyone can remember the first dean of the University of North Carolina School of Nursing. She was a great lady and leader to all who were privileged to be part of her dream."

During the following years, members of the first class established their individual families and careers, and they became solid citizens of an adult world. Each year, the School of Nursing updated alumni on their classmates by sending them the quarterly newsletter, *The Messenger*. Individually, the members of the class of 1955 kept in touch, but it was not until their thirtieth anniversary in 1985 that time allowed for another reunion.

For their thirtieth reunion, there were no formal ceremonies, but rather a reception and dinner at the plush Europa Hotel was arranged by some of the class members. "It was an elegant evening of cocktails, dinner, and much conversation," recalls Janet. "There were thirteen members of the class and eight spouses, so twenty-one in attendance. We were enjoying being together so much that Geri and Bob invited us to their home in Chapel Hill to continue our fun. It was a very nostalgic, wonderful evening." Sally wrote a poem about the occasion.

Thirty Years
By Sally Winn Nicholson

Thirty years ago we parted the Class of 1955—First Class.
Thirty-four years ago we met
Could it possibly be that long?
At eighteen, did we ever think
    We'd ever be fifty-two?
    grandmothers?
    teachers?
    returning here?
The time so long
    so short
So much has happened
    to us
    to Nursing
And we remember
    Smith Hall
    living in North Carolina Memorial Hospital
    the "new" dorm
    men we dated—loved
Names come to mind
    Dean Kemble
    Professors
    Friends
Places we loved—or didn't love
    Wilson Library
    The Monogram Club
    The Rendezvous Room
    Lenoir Hall

So many faces gone
We greet each other
    "You look great"
    "Not changed"
    "Well, maybe the gray hair is new"
    mostly "I'm so glad to see you"
We've all changed so much
    done so much
    lived through so much
There are goals met
    and unmet
Those we've loved
    and lost
This is a time for remembering
    and for looking ahead
    for laughter
    and tears
It is personal—professional
Nursing, changing
    Process
    Diagnosis
    Independent practice
    Theories
Nursing, unchanging
    Responsibility
    Scientific base
    Caring
Of all of the things in our lives
    the profession binds us together
Whether we practice or not
    We are nurses

Whatever else we do
    This is where we began
    Together
And the young ones think
    "Will we ever be THAT OLD?"
Graduates (and graduate students)
    born since we left
    to whom Korea exists mainly in history
    Vietnam is hazy
    our fashions "in" again
This school our common ground
    History made and being made
We have changed and are changing
    the fabric of Nursing
Where will they take it?

Donna initiated the next gathering when she nominated Bette for the School of Nursing 1992 Alumna of the Year Award. After Bette was selected as the recipient, Donna wrote to their classmates, asking them to meet in Chapel Hill to bask in the glory of Bette's award on September 19. Janet recalls that it was a most memorable occasion, as they celebrated and congratulated Bette for her award. "How proud we were that she received this prestigious award for her contribution, dedication, and accomplishments to the nursing profession," she says.

The alumni award recognized Bette for exemplifying the role that nurses can play in caring for patients, advancing the nursing profession, and improving health care. Bette was making a difference in the profession by taking her Nurses Organization of Veterans Affairs (NOVA) work, and her Chapel Hill nursing education, to Capitol Hill. Cynthia M. Freund, dean of the School of Nursing in 1992, remarked that people like Bette were helping nursing to gain the respect that it deserves. She added that Bette ex-

1992 Alumna of the Year, Bette Davis, with Dean Freund.

hibits excellence not only in psychiatric liaison nursing, but also as a spokesperson of the profession.

Bette says that receiving this award from her school and peers was the highlight of her nursing career. "Nursing's image has always suffered a lack of definition," she says. "The nursing profession has never been given enough credit for the caliber of people in the profession or for what is required to be a nurse. I'm glad to say that's changing, and I'm proud to think I may have a part in that change."

Members of the class joined Bette's friends as well as School of Nursing students, faculty, and alumni—a total of 150 people—for a day of activities. The ceremony took place on the lawn of the School of Nursing on Alumni Day during football season. "It was one of those famous Chapel Hill days with a Carolina-blue sky, the sounds of the Bell Tower chimes, the UNC marching band making their way to Kenan Stadium, and students (young and old) cheering on the Tar Heels," Janet says. "As we gathered together, hugging, talking, and laughing, everyone could definitely detect the genuine love and camaraderie that were so apparent. As always, past years seemed to fade—insignificant were the gray strands of hair, the few extra pounds, and even a wrinkle or two. We saw the young girls we met in 1951. We especially enjoyed being with Bette on her special day—one of our own, who so richly deserved all the accolades associated with this esteemed honor."

At dinner that evening, talk turned to writing their class history. In October, Bette received a letter from Joy in which she wrote, "I'm working on some ideas for a '1955 Nursing School Booklet'—our personal stories, viewpoints, and anecdotes. What were you doing when you first heard about Dean Kemble's new bachelor of science in nursing program at UNC? And where were you?"

Within a year they were moving on this idea. Dr. Lud Scott, a nephew of Elizabeth Scott Carrington, generously gave Mary some copies of a book called *The School of Nursing at the University of North Carolina in Chapel Hill and the Pioneers Who Built It* for her to send to class members. In this book, author Gayle Lane Fitzgerald documented the history of the School of Nursing with a focus on the dedicated supporters, administrators, and faculty who contributed to its formation.

Janet and Joy gathered ideas and information for a book that would tell the collective stories of the first class of nurses to graduate from UNC Chapel Hill. Janet sent out questionnaires to the classmates, requesting information about why they decided to come to the School of Nursing, particular memories, and

Sara and Don, Joy and Larry, and Donna and Brantley at Donna's house in Santa Fe in 1993.

other general ideas. Some classmates sent Janet and Joy written papers about their undergraduate years at Carolina or anecdotal material, which Janet and Joy met to work on from time to time during the next two years.

In September, 1993, several of them met in Santa Fe, New Mexico, where Donna and Brantley have a home. Donna promised to organize margaritas, art galleries, great eats, great weather, Indian pueblos, and a couple of working sessions. Bette, Joy and Larry, Sara and Don, and of course Donna and Brantley had a fabulous time doing all of the above—except any writing. However, they did photocopy many papers to share with the others.

Janet recalls that not all their classmates were as enthusiastic as they had hoped, and the idea of the book was put on hold. However, they kept all the information they had gathered, somehow knowing it would be needed at a later time.

The class of 1955 celebrated its fortieth reunion with a brunch at The Carolina Inn. Dr. Eloise Lewis, one of the school's original faculty members, was able to join them for the event. Seated: Gwen, Winnie, Martha, Janet, Joy, Sally, Louise. Standing: Gloria, Sara, Mary, Bette, Donna, Eloise Lewis, Geri, Arlene.

The class of 1955 attended two events in 1995. In May, they enjoyed the UNC General Alumni Association Class of 1955 Fortieth Reunion. Gloria coordinated activities for this reunion, which included an afternoon concert by the Glenn Miller Orchestra. Later, they met at the reunion banquet. Bette recalls, "After the program, we went dancing to the music of the Doug Clark and the Hot Nuts band with two younger men from the class of 1960 I had picked up while on the bus to the banquet. A third one joined us once the fun began."

Later that year, they attended the School of Nursing's Alumni Day and Reunion Day on September 30 at Carrington Hall to celebrate forty years since graduation. Most classmates attended with their spouses and family members. Winnie, Louise, and Mary coordinated the day's activities, which included brunch at The Carolina Inn, a class photo, a football game, and a tour of Carrington Hall. The day concluded with a dinner and program at a local hotel, where they enjoyed displays of their student uniforms and other historical memorabilia.

"We simply were thrilled to be with each other again," Bette says. "Many photos were taken of this happy group—all smiling—all evening."

Every member of the nursing class of 1955 contributed to the School of Nursing as part of the UNC Bicentennial and Annual Fund Campaign that concluded on June 30, 1995. The donations from the class were given in memory of their classmate Virginia Edwards Coupe, who died of cancer on January 9, 1995. Rae wrote that she remembers the ease with which Virginia wrote so well, finishing case studies in half the time it took the rest of us—and better written. "We cherish her memory as a friend and member of our class," Bette says.

Over the forty years that had elapsed since graduation, members of the class of 1955 had grown families, developed careers, traveled the world, and advanced the nursing profession. Despite their busy lives, they always made time to gather back in Chapel Hill to reminisce and catch up with each other.

9

Later Career and Family

As time progressed, families and careers grew for the class of 1955. Nurses with BSNs were rare, and having the bachelor's degree led to many opportunities for the graduates. Several members of the class were invited to teach and to help develop nursing programs.

In August of 1965, Gloria was contacted about a teaching position for practical nurses at Lee County Industrial Education Center in Sanford, North Carolina. "I wanted a part-time position, but they needed a full-time person, so I told them I would consider it. They called back and said they had hired someone for the job. I was relieved, as I wanted to spend more time with our four young children. The day after Labor Day, the college called

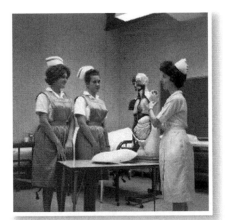

Gloria Peele (right) speaks with two nursing students during one of the first classes she taught in 1966.

because they were desperate to replace the lady they hired, who had quit after one day. I went to the school that afternoon for an interview, met the other nursing instructor, and signed on for the position full time. Two days later I was in the classroom."

Gloria was one of two instructors for the twenty practical nursing students at Lee County Industrial Education Center. The other instructor was the director of the program and a graduate of Rex Hospital School of Nursing, which Gloria heard about nearly every day for twenty years. The director taught the medical and surgical classes, while Gloria taught anatomy and physiology, pharmacology, maternity nursing, and pediatrics.

"Almost every night during the first quarter, I dreamed something dreadful would happen—not being prepared, the bell never ringing, being late for class, etc.," says Gloria. "Gradually, I calmed down and loved my new position. It was fun learning with the students and working with them in the hospital setting with the patients. We were 'hands-on' instructors."

After one year of working full time, Gloria began working part time to be home with her children in the afternoon. Her hours were 8:00 a.m. to noon five days a week, with clinical instruction for three of those mornings. In 1970, she returned full time and continued until 1981.

Nancy Matthews Hall, a UNC SON graduate with an MSN, was hired to develop a two-year associate-degree program. "We developed and wrote competencies while teaching full time," Gloria says. "I told Nancy, I would rather be digging ditches than writing." The two-year program began in September, 1982, and the college hired two more staff members and a secretary. "We were off campus at the time while a nursing building was being built. The independence from administration was delightful. We were back on campus sometime during 1985."

In 1964, Craven Technical Institute approached Winnie about helping them start an LPN program under the auspices of the Lenoir County Industrial Education Center. However, she declined because she had two young children. In 1969, they asked her again, and this time, she accepted. The school needed a nurse with a BSN, and there were only five in the area.

"I taught with Craven Community College for twenty-one years in the licensed practical nursing program and some in the associate degree of nursing program when that was later added. I also served as program director of the licensed practical nursing program for approximately ten years."

Winnie retired in 1990 due to a fractured knee, and within the year was caring for her husband and mother.

Winnie Cotton (right) pins a member of the class of 1984 at Craven Community College.

"While still employed, I assisted in caring for my father, who had Alzheimer's disease," Winnie says. "All of my family members were cared for at home, and I am grateful for the knowledge to care for them, allowing them to be content at home."

In 2007, the nurse in charge of the operating-room team for Winnie's cardiac surgery was a former student, as were several of the staff in the Cardiac Intermediate Care Unit and the Rehabilitation Unit at Craven Regional Medical Center in New Bern, North Carolina. "When teaching, I used to tell the students that I wanted to teach them to give good nursing care because some day I might be their patient," Winnie says. "I have always enjoyed seeing that many of my former students continued their education and were in significant nursing positions."

In 1970, Wayne Community College in Goldsboro, North Carolina, established a two-year nursing program, which Pat helped organize. She wrote and implemented much of the curriculum in the beginning and was an instructor there for fourteen years.

"Since moving to Cary, North Carolina, I have been active in numerous volunteer and civic organizations," Pat says. "While serving on scholarship committees for several of these groups, I have had the opportunity to help local individuals further their education, many of them seeking careers in nursing."

Pat Johnson, 1982.

By 1965, Donna and Brantley had three children and had lived in the United States for several years. They were living in San Antonio, and a major commercial airline hired Brantley as a pilot. "During their first year of employment, the airline industry tests their pilots in many ways," Donna recalls. "For example, Brantley's monthly salary was only $500. With three little children and a mortgage, I needed no greater incentive to go to work."

Donna applied for a position at the School of Nursing at Incarnate Word College (now Incarnate Word University) in San Antonio and was hired the same day. Donna was a coteacher with Sister Olivia for maternal and child health. "She was a delightful Irish nun, and I was responsible for teaching the pediatrics portion of the course," Donna says. "Having not looked at a pediatrics textbook in ten years was torment enough, but I also had to find reliable help for child care and housekeeping. With Brantley not there to even talk about these things, I felt responsible for everything twenty-four/seven."

Donna clearly remembers one morning when she was driving to Santa Rosa Hospital in downtown San Antonio, where the students did their clinical. "I remember thinking such thoughts as, 'Suppose my car has trouble and I don't make it,' and other scenarios that would not hold water. When I arrived and met Sister Olivia, who was unflappable, I said to her, 'I think I'm having a sinking spell,' meaning 'I don't think I can do this.' With an easy smile and twinkling blue eyes, she said, 'Well, I'll do it for you.' Within two heartbeats a different feeling washed over me, and I instantly felt confident that not only could I do this; I would. Just knowing that someone would cover for me gave confidence."

Santa Rosa was a large downtown hospital with an extensive pediatrics service. At the time, it served three main population groups: Caucasian, Hispanic, and the military. In the pediatric hospital two disorders were prevalent: pneumonia in the winter and diarrhea and dehydration (D&D) in the summer. "Working there gave me an opportunity to learn about another culture and their belief system, and I drew on those experiences years later in medical anthropology. Geri and Bob were also stationed in San Antonio, and Geri, too, had worked at Santa Rosa."

Donna taught at Incarnate Word until they moved to Dallas in 1967. Donna then enrolled in a course in cardiovascular nursing at the Dallas campus of Texas Woman's University. "There I met some nurses and quickly knew that I wanted to continue working," Donna recalls.

Bette lived near Donna and Brantley while she worked at Dallas VA Medical Center. "How wonderful it was to meet up with my roommate from UNC," says Donna. "Sally was also in Dallas and introduced me to her friend Martha Bradley."

Martha was instrumental in Donna's decision to interview for a position at Texas Woman's College. "I seriously considered the teaching position they offered me at Texas Woman's College but was also intrigued by a position at Children's Medical Center, which was affiliated with Southwestern Medical School. Children's Medical Center was in a new building and also had a new director of nursing, Trude Aufhauser."

Donna accepted the position at Children's Medical Center because of Ms. Aufhauser's enthusiasm about pediatric nursing. "She was progressive in practice, encouraged my innovative ideas, and supported me in everything that I wanted to do. She was an ideal director."

Donna took on a new position that Ms. Aufhauser created to focus on nurse education and clinical practice. The position included coordinating clinical practice for the four nursing schools with clinical rotations at Children's Medical Center. "My first project was to develop a written care-plan record that the primary nurse initiated upon patient admission," Donna says. "A longtime volunteer generously funded the printing of a large folded index card used for this record."

The nurses' aides at that time were adult black women who had worked at the Children's Hospital before the new building was complete. These ladies wore pink-striped pinafores and had relied on primarily "on the job" training in addition to their own personal and extensive experiences as mothers.

"With the director's approval, I sought to reframe perceptions and enhance skill levels," Donna recalls. "I wanted this vital and dedicated group to have uniforms that befitted adult women, and they collectively selected a soft mint-green uniform. Additionally, they enrolled in a Red Cross nursing course. Upon completion, Ms. Aufhauser presided over a ceremony at which they wore their new uniforms and were formally recognized and presented their certificates."

Orientation for new volunteers was also under Donna's purview. Volunteers were a vital part of the hospital. They would do things such as transport children to X-ray or other departments in big red wagons, and manage library carts that held books for parents and patients to check out. During orientation, the volunteers learned about Children's Medical Center's philosophy for excellent family- and child-centered care for hospitalized children.

Donna also attended the First National Pediatric Intensive Care Seminar, sponsored by Southwestern Medical School and Children's Medical Center, and then became the coordinator for the next two annual national seminars.

Arlene and Dr. Thurstone had two sons and one daughter, and they had been married for fifty years when he died in 2005. He was a leader in the field of ultrasound holography. Arlene Morgan Thurstone died in November, 2012.

Arlene Thurstone, 1995.

In most cases, the class of 1955 had no problems obtaining nursing jobs. Their degree opened opportunities for leadership positions, and their UNC training gave them the tools to take on challenges.

By 1974, Gwen had five children, their drugstore was doing well, and a new nursing home was being built in Tryon, North Carolina. In addition to Gwen's husband, the drugstore had a second pharmacist whose wife was a nurse too.

"We decided it was time to get back to nursing, and we were both hired by the nursing home," Gwen says. The nursing home was a sixty-skilled-bed facility, and within only six weeks Gwen became the director of nursing, and her friend became the RN in charge of the facility.

The facility was one of a chain of eight nursing homes. It had apartments, which they checked and helped keep occupied. Soon the facility added thirty more beds. "I enjoyed this thoroughly," recalls Gwen. "I did the scheduling, directed the monthly staff meetings, checked residents daily, and if possible, met with their families. Plus, we had regular survey visits from state representatives, who checked policies and procedures and how they were followed."

Gwen Butler at the nursing home in Tryon, North Carolina.

In 1982, Gwen took an administrative course and transferred to Shelby, North Carolina, to become the administrator of a 160-bed nursing home owned by the same company as the nursing homes at which she had been working. This facility had sixty skilled beds and one hundred intermediate beds. "I had a great staff and truly enjoyed my eleven years at this facility, even though to get there I drove fifty miles each way on crooked roads. The state survey team became more involved each year and expected so much paperwork. It became difficult to spend quality time with the residents."

After eleven years as nursing-home administrator, Gwen retired and began caring for her and her husband's parents, his aunt and uncle, and the grandchildren. "Our life has been good; our only daughter is a pharmacist and owns our drugstore along with her husband, who is also a pharmacist. Our four sons are also doing well. Three live in Tryon, and one is in Apex, North Carolina. We have thirteen grandchildren and six more by marriage."

In 1978, Janet returned to full-time nursing at Chapel Hill Obstetrics and Gynecology. Her parents had retired, and Bill had moved to his profession in hospital administration. He had a very successful career in the long-term-care arena. Chapel Hill Obstetrics and Gynecology was a private practice of four doctors. Two of them were graduates of UNC School of Medicine and had taken classes from the same instructors as Janet. Dr. William Nebel, the senior physician, had been mentored by the famous and memorable Dr. Robert Ross, who was the OB-GYN chief of staff at North Carolina Memorial Hospital for many years.

"Although I had not been working for a few years, the training and experience from nursing school proved to be a solid background in all the skills I needed," Janet recalls. The RN, especially with a degree, was known at that time as a nurse clinician, carrying out an extension of the physician's workload. At Chapel Hill OB-GYN, patients could have minor surgeries, diagnostic biopsies, tests for early detection of pregnancy and for abnormalities, fertility procedures to aid conception, ultrasounds, and even amniocentesis. The two RNs also offered Lamaze and early-pregnancy classes, consultation, and counseling.

The doctors made daily visits to the hospital to review the progress of patients. After the doctor visited, one of the RNs would visit with each patient to answer medical questions and address personal issues or concerns, including ones tied to situations that might arise after discharge. The nurse prepared and gave all the discharge instructions, and followed up with a telephone call each day for a week, noting changes or other information in a progress report.

The doctors were inundated with stacks of charts for patients who needed telephone calls returned, so they commissioned Janet's assistance to determine the medical issue, offer advice, and help with a solution. "I did just that, and soon the patients began to call me instead of the physician, knowing I would give them an answer—either myself or consult with the doctor for instructions. This

Janet Littlejohn, 1989.

169

afforded the physician more time for patient care, yet offered continuity when patients called with questions or concerns. Talking with the nurse often seemed to help allay many of the fears associated with pregnancy. We had been well trained to *listen*, and give patients a comforting solution in any situation."

The doctors were confident with Janet's knowledge and ability and her genuine concern for patients, so the telephone became an important and integral part of patient care. Janet was essentially acting as a triage nurse, a title that arose around this time.

In 1985, Bill received a promotion that took them to the small village of Clemmons in the Winston-Salem area. "I really missed Chapel Hill and my work there, especially as I interviewed for jobs and could find nothing in the OB-GYN area. As I believe everything happens for a reason, my next endeavor proved even more interesting and challenging."

Janet joined the practice of Dr. Jaime Trujillo, who was in internal medicine with a specialty in endocrinology. "I was back in general medicine, and it had changed," she recalls. "Knowledge I had not used in many years came into focus once again: physical signs and symptoms along with diagnostic tests and new medications. So my new pastime evolved into reading medical books, journals, and periodicals to enhance my familiarity with this new specialty."

The treatment of diabetes had significantly changed since Janet was in school. Diagnosis was earlier thanks to the frequent lab tests that took place during routine examinations. Machines to test blood sugar had gone from laptop-size to pocket- and pen-size, and injection equipment was smaller and disposable. "Patients required constant instructions on these new, unprecedented tools," Janet recalls. "The nursing staff offered diabetic education and dietary classes. During my tenure there, we were accredited for this instruction, and a new name was chosen,

The Salem Center. It became the second largest practice for diabetes in North Carolina."

Although diabetes was the primary focus of the practice, thyroid dysfunction was the second most prominent disease seen at the center. "I remembered my thyroidectomy-patient case study from the surgical rotation during nursing school," Janet recalls. "The current treatment, involving scans, biopsies, and radioactive iodine, has made treatment for thyroid cancer much simpler. Myasthenia gravis, which was involved in my medical-rotation case study, was also in the endocrinology field, and that too has experienced many treatment advances."

Internal medicine required constant care. All the organs of the body were monitored and medications changed often, as new, more effective ones were indicated. "I never stopped learning, as I worked for a very dedicated physician," Janet says. "I joined Dr. Trujillo's office as the only registered nurse, but the staff grew with the growing practice. He employed only RNs, and I often assisted in their training and indoctrination into the preferred procedures. Eventually, I authored a procedure manual for continuity of care, and also prepared booklets for staff and patients."

Dr. Trujillo had an extremely impressive policy to telephone patients the day after their visit to discuss lab tests, scans, biopsies, and other test results and to give follow-up instructions. He reviewed each chart before passing it on to Janet so that she could call the patient. Janet also fielded incoming calls, assisting the patient or conferring with Dr. Trujillo.

"Charting every conversation was most important—just as we had been instructed several years ago," Janet says. "Many patients became inclined to call me for advice, so *again*, my listening skills were put to the test. I always tried to follow through with the knowledge and education instilled in us as young nursing students along with my years of experience. Coupled with genuine care and concern for my patients, I found this portion of my nursing career to be extremely rewarding. In 2005, I retired from full-time nursing, yet I still work part time occasionally, and enjoy it just as I have in years past."

In August of 1969, Sara and her husband returned to the United States, along with their four children. She worked in public health in the state of New York, and when they relocated to Vermont, she accepted the position of assistant director of nursing with the Rutland Area Visiting

Sara Flynn with her children in 1969.

Nurses Association. However, she again felt the pull of global nursing. In 1982, Sara and her husband formed an international health-consulting firm, and they made their home in Brussels, Belgium, until 1997.

While in Belgium, Sara enrolled in the nursing program at the Institute of Tropical Medicine in Antwerp, Belgium. The curriculum consisted of courses in tropical pathology and epidemiology, hematology, protozoology, entomology, helminthology, bacteriology, maternal and child health care in the tropics, and public health care principles in tropical regions.

"The course work was a real challenge, not only in content, but also because it was given in French," she remembers. "I was not sure if I could handle the language. I also discovered the difference between European and American university teaching methods. We had five months of lectures and laboratory work, two weeks to review, and then the final exams, which constituted our entire grade. Including the travel time from Brussels to Antwerp, these were twelve-hour days, five days a week for five months—quite a challenge for a fifty-five-year-old student having to function in a foreign language. I loved it."

She received her diploma and certification in tropical nursing in 1987. "There were many French-speaking European and African nurses in this program who failed to pass and were not qualified. I was delighted to graduate 'avec distinction.' I attribute my success to the nursing education I received at the UNC School of Nursing and my ten years of experience in the Middle East."

Two years later, she became cochair of Nurses Abroad, a group formed under the auspices of the Foreign American Women's Clubs Overseas to address the needs of American and other English-speaking nurses living in Belgium. Many expatriate nurses were not allowed to work in Belgium. Nurses had to be a resident of a European country in order to work in Belgium. "Each year nurses arrived with great expectations of working in a foreign culture, only to be completely frustrated by the situation," Sara says.

Nurses Abroad provided its members with information about the Belgian health-care system, peer support and networking, and a newsletter with information about educational opportunities. Sara was responsible for the group's monthly newsletter.

Sara and her husband retired in 1997 and returned to Vermont, where they dedicated their time to family life. After fighting a twenty-month battle against cancer, Sara Catherine Blaylock Flynn died in October, 2008.

In 1961, Martha's husband joined a classmate to open a practice in the small town of Warrenton, North Carolina. "I answered the phone at night, on weekends, and when my husband was on house calls." Their third child, Mark, then arrived. After four years and the loss of a medical partner, they moved to Sanford, North Carolina, in 1965 and had their fourth child, Caroline.

Martha participated in various civic functions and other activities that promoted medicine and public health to the public. "I utilized my bridge club, civic meetings, church work, and friends to interpret and teach about conditions, procedures, and medications. I became respected for my own health knowledge and care," she says.

Martha and her husband spent some time traveling in many countries around the world, enjoying learning about the medical care and culture of other countries, and also enjoying scenery and architecture. In the fall of 2013, Martha was hospitalized at UNC Hospital, where two students from the School of Nursing had the opportunity to care for her. She told them, "You are the best nurses, because you don't just learn how to do things at Carolina, you learn why you do them." Martha Evelyn Yount Cline died on September 28, 2013.

Joy moved to New Orleans in 1974. "We entered a whole new world—Cajun Country! The atmosphere, cuisine, and especially the music endear this area to me forever. Even now, when I hear the Cajun music, I feel like 'dancing in the street,' a common practice there."

In 1980, Joy returned to Charlotte with her daughters and ended her marriage. She joined hospice care as a hospice nurse and became reacquainted with old friends in Charlotte. "One of these friends became my soul mate and husband for more than twenty years, until his death in year 2003," Joy says. "Lawrence and I traveled a lot—to more than nineteen countries, were step-parents to each other's children, and restored and decorated houses. His hobbies included making furniture. Mine included flower arrangements, forty-five-plus years with the Garden Club, and creative writing."

In the early nineties, Joy participated in Margaret G. Bigger's courses on preserving stories in writing and began publishing her true-experience memories with other class members in paperback booklets that were in demand at bookstores all over Charlotte. The most recent booklet, *Gray Haired Grins & Giggles*, was published in October, 1995, and was into its fourth printing by June, 1996. "In the fall of 1995 at Chapel Hill's University Mall, I autographed copies of the book, a compilation of 160 humorous life-experiences told by forty-five senior authors," Joy says. "I wrote six of the book's tales, including one about my nursing-school-entrance physical exam titled "Mortification."

The university stressed the importance of community involvement, and that principle greatly impacted and enriched the lives of Rae and her husband. In Huntsville, Alabama, the pay scale for nurses was so low that it did not cover the expenses of child care. "Ed had developed a business relationship with the school superintendent, and when the system was looking for a chemistry teacher, Ed mentioned my Carolina training, and I was asked to apply," recalls Rae.

Rae at age forty-five.

"Fortunately, our four-year, two-summer experience was so comprehensive that I was qualified and was employed as a chemistry teacher at Huntsville High School."

Huntsville established programs of hospice, and later, Hospice Cares, which provided services to patients in the final stages of illness at some cost. "I served on the boards for both and came to realize our responsibility was fundraising and not patient care," Rae says. In 1999, a friend who was also a nurse recognized that patients with

175

long-term illnesses also needed services. "Five of us started Friends, Inc., a nonprofit organization that provides volunteer support to patients with serious illnesses," Rae says. "We served eighty-five patients in 2011."

Rae says that she has always loved to read, and she worked with the local library for several years, cochairing its annual fundraising dinner for two years. She has loved tennis since high school. "I remember having to wear raincoats over our tennis shorts as we walked to the university's courts," Rae recalls. "Tennis is still a passion, and I play regularly." She was ranked number four in Alabama before her first knee surgery, and she held many offices in the local Women's Tennis Association.

Rae's husband, Ed, has always loved politics and education. When Huntsville changed to an elected board of education, he ran for the office, won, and served fourteen years on the board, twelve years as its president. He also served as president of the state board and was instrumental in winning legislative support for public kindergartens in Alabama in the 1970s.

While in high school Ed loved guiding visiting relatives through the National Gallery of Art. His deep appreciation of art gave Rae an idea for a Christmas present in 1988, after Ed decided to step down from the board of education. "I gave him a series of lessons with a locally published art instructor," she says. "That gift completely changed our lives."

Rae (right), her husband, Ed, and Dean Cronenwett with one of Ed's painting. This was one of two paintings that they donated to the School of Nursing in 2004.

Ed fell in love with the act of painting and retired early to spend the rest of his life with a paintbrush in his hand. More than 1600 of Ed's paintings were selected for private, public, corporate, university, and museum collections in the United States, Europe, and Asia. Ed painted *The First Ladies' Garden*, which was commissioned by the White House Historical Association and hangs in the White House Visitor Center.

"Art expanded our world," Rae says. "For fifteen years we spent a month each year in 'art rambles' throughout Europe. Ed gathered material for potential paintings, and the two of us enjoyed daily life in France, Italy, England, Spain, and other countries. Each trip included at least a week in Paris, and it became our favorite city to walk the boulevards, eat casual bistro lunches, enjoy great art museums, and delight in evenings of concerts, ballet performances, and long dinners."

After leaving the board of education, Ed was the chair of the City of Huntsville Planning Commission and also served on the board of trustees for the Alabama School of Fine Arts in Birmingham. "My family, church, community service, and tennis have been the cornerstones of my life and all connect back to my classmates and those wonderful days we spent together at Chapel Hill," Rae says.

10

Graduate School and New Opportunities

The class of 1955 understood the importance of high quality nursing education, and several members of the first class continued their education with master's and doctoral degrees.

After Gloria helped Nancy Matthews Hall develop the new two-year program at Lee County Industrial Education Center, now called Central Carolina Technical College, Nancy encouraged her to begin a master's degree.

"I told her no, as I felt my life was full and I did not see the need for further education." Nancy persisted until Gloria finally enrolled part time in the master in health occupation program at North Carolina State University. She began evening classes in January, 1983. In May of 1985, Nancy resigned and Dr. Marvin Joyner, the president of the college, asked Gloria to become the director. "I took the summer off, enrolled full time in the master's program, and became director in September, 1985."

In the ten years that Gloria directed the associate degree nursing program, she oversaw the launch of two satellite programs for practical nursing in neighboring counties and a new evening/weekend program for LPNs. The school also began to accept LPNs to its second-level program for progression to the associate degree. "Needless to say, I became closely involved with the North Carolina State Board of Nursing. This was truly a challenge, but I developed a new respect for the board members. My advisor on the board was always very willing to assist me or answer my questions."

Don retired in February, 1995, and Gloria retired in November, 1995. "For ten years I volunteered as the secretary for an organization that drove patients to radiation treatments, and then I transitioned to being a scheduler one month of the year. We continue to be active in church and enjoy our beach house in North Carolina's Emerald Isle."

Of the twenty-eight master's students admitted to Yale School of Nursing in fall of 1969, twelve, including Bette, entered the psychiatric nursing program. About half of the twelve had just received undergraduate nursing degrees, and the rest had some nursing experience. Bette received a US Public Health Service Grant that paid her tuition and a small monthly stipend for each of the two academic years.

"Looking back, I remain amazed at the remarkable teachers who recognized my

Bette Davis, 1969.

potential, gave me a chance, and nourished me," Bette recalls. "Their mentorship would later enable me to mentor others."

When Bette entered Yale, it was a time of historic student unrest across the country. In the late 1960s, organized protests were escalated by the assassinations of Martin Luther King and Robert Kennedy, discontent over the Vietnam War, civil rights, and community issues. Urban rampages burst out in cities around the nation, especially in Washington, DC. "As the fall of 1969 began, I did not anticipate that events on Yale campus and in New Haven would have such an impact on the country and me," Bette says.

In the spring of 1970 a Black Panther chapter in New Haven merged with radicals in a massive protest leading to the May Day weekend demonstration. As ten thousand to twenty thousand demonstrators converged on the New Haven Green, Yale president Kingman Brewster took the unorthodox step of welcoming demonstrators to Yale. He asked for a policy of openness, and for faculty to be free to suspend classes. The rally's organizers preached nonviolence and made love speeches. The peaceful messages worked.

"Yale housed and fed the demonstrators, and the medical and nurse students—including me—manned first-aid tents," Bette recalls. "It was phenomenal to be present at this demonstration. I was awake most of the night before, as trucks of reservists rolled down the highway next to my apartment.

As a new student, Bette enrolled in Dean Margaret Arnstein's class on issues in health fields related to nursing. "The class required a term paper, and Dean Arnstein liked my topic of 'Community Control and Nursing Involvement,' but suggested I should challenge the solutions offered in the literature, include my own opinion, and think more independently and critically."

Another inspiring nursing great at Yale was Virginia Henderson, an early definer of nursing as having a separate and independent role in providing health care. She was compiling the first annotated index of nursing research called the *Nursing Studies Index*.

"I was thrilled to meet her, and she, also, was delighted to discuss her research and demonstrate her method of using three-by-five index cards for annotating a bibliography. One of my nursing keepsakes is an autographed copy of her small book, *The Nature of Nursing: A Definition and Its Implications for Practice, Research, and Education*. First published in 1966, it is a treasure that speaks to the evolvement of professional nursing and its function. To me, she represented the epitome of nursing. I cherished my time with her and appreciated that she made herself available to students, even after graduation."

For clinical experience, Bette was assigned to the Connecticut Mental Health Center's twenty-two-bed research unit for social psychology and psychiatry. This unit integrated individual and group psychotherapy with community psychiatry.

Bette met Rhetaugh Dumas, associate professor and chairperson of the psychiatric nursing program and director of nursing in the Connecticut Mental Health Center, when the twelve students entering the psychiatric nursing program were introduced to members of the psychiatric nursing faculty. "Rhetaugh, seated and comfortable, spoke of her ideas and guidance for us in a warm, informal manner."

Later, Bette attended a national community-leaders' conference that Dumas led at Yale. Graduate nursing students and nursing faculty from schools on the East Coast along with community leaders representing New Haven attended the conference, which dealt with confrontational issues and offered opportunities to learn how to work with others in small and large groups.

Rhetaugh's leadership shaped conditions for several hundred of the conference attendees to follow her to President Brewster's office with requests for changes in the community. "Before that happy ending, though, there was a whole day when we all sat silently, frozen with guilt, feeling forced to listen to speeches and comments from black community members and leaders, who were controlling the conference," Bette remembers. "That is, until I had had enough and stood in line for a turn at the microphone. When I got the microphone, the community-leader speaker grabbed it from me. With my knees knocking and voice trembling, I took it back and said, 'We listened to you, now you should listen to us,' at which point, he agreed. I spoke, and a line formed behind me for others to be heard. I can't remember one word of what I said, but I got to say it."

Rhetaugh, an African American woman, was proud of Bette and repeatedly brought the incident up during their work together over the next twenty-five years. "One of her main interests was developing leadership in nurses, and she wrote and spoke on the subject for the rest of her life," Bette says. "Years later she participated in the Nurses Organization of Veterans Affairs (NOVA), first as a speaker, and later, when I was a leader in NOVA, I recruited her as a member of the VA Commission on the Future Structure of Veterans Health Care. She later was a consultant on diversity for the UNC School of Nursing faculty soon after Dean Cronenwett arrived."

For her master's thesis, Bette tested the effectiveness of three different nursing approaches in relieving patients' pain. The three treatment groups or approaches were operationally defined by Donna Diers's interaction analysis, the Nurse Orientation System. Bette replicated clinical experiments first conducted by Angela McBride, then by Ruth Schmidt. "I became the third investigator for the same study that was repeated three times with three different nurses over five years." Bette says. "Replicated clinical research on the effects of direct patient care was rare. I liked the idea of providing additional evidence to guide clinical practice."

Together, the three studies added evidence that even when the differences among the three treatment groups were not statistically significant, most of the patients, regardless of group assignment, were judged to feel better, though not as much as when they were also treated as feeling and thinking persons, not just as physical beings.[8]

"All too soon graduation arrived in June, 1971, sixteen years after my first graduation in 1955 as a Carolina nurse," Bette says. "Again, I can say I had the best education, experienced a closeness with the faculty, and enjoyed the friendship of smart and rare classmates, all for which I am blessed and thankful. I had a chance to grow some more, as much was given to me, this time as a Yale nurse."

Upon completing her master's in community health nursing at Emory University, Sally had hoped to teach at Emory School of Nursing. However, the school did not offer her a position. Her advisor, Nan Springstead, met Dr. Faye Pannell of the Texas Woman's University in Dallas, who offered Sally the position of instructor of public health nursing there.

Sally and her sister drove to Dallas in August, 1961. "It was a very hot trip since my 1959 Chevrolet did not have an air conditioner," she recalls. "It took three days with stops in Montgomery, Alabama, and Shreveport, Louisiana. Dallas would be my home for the next three years."

Sally was at Parkland Hospital in Dallas for clinical the day that President Kennedy was shot. He was raced there by ambulance, with sirens blaring and accompanied by a speeding convoy of police cars. She had gone to her classroom to set up her teaching audiovisuals, and when she entered, only a few students and physicians were in the room. They were standing at the windows overlooking the entrance to the ER. Some of her students were nurses who worked in the ER, and they had gone down to check the schedule and see what was going on.

The scene at Parkland Hospital on November 22, 1963, was like no other. The flurry of activities and the shocking and unbelievable magnitude of what had just transpired surrounding the president's assassination were surreal. Jackie Kennedy's steadfast presence in her bloodstained pink suit as Lyndon Johnson was sworn in as president, and the swiftness with which the whole entourage flew off in Air Force One left an aura that blanketed the whole country, and even the world.

"What a strange few weeks followed. My classroom became the pressroom, and my grade book disappeared. I figured some student or students had taken the opportunity to get rid of grades they didn't like."

Sally began to realize that if she was to support herself with a career in education, then she needed to get a doctorate. "I would get little support for this plan from my dean, because she would fear that this would cause her to lose a faculty member."

In 1964, Sally began preparations to leave Dallas. She considered positions as a public health consultant with the Georgia Health Department as well as two possible faculty positions at the School of Nursing in Chapel Hill—either teaching pediatric nursing or teaching in the new graduate program between the School of Public Health and the School of Nursing. "I had been teaching pediatric nursing in the summers, when public health nursing wasn't taught," Sally says.

She was hired at the School of Nursing to teach with the pediatrics section for the maternal-child group, and she began teaching in the fall of 1965. She was also responsible for the small hospital course in Smithfield, North Carolina, that was being phased out that year, and was part of the team teaching a course in community health with graduate students.

During Sally's second year at UNC, she began the application process for the graduate program in the Institute of Child Study at the University of Maryland School of Nursing. "Dean Kemble helped me secure a scholarship from the Southern Association of Schools of Nursing," Sally says. This scholarship was named for Sally's friends, Dr. and Mrs. Bixler, who were patrons of art in Atlanta and had lost their lives in a tragic Paris plane crash. Sally was the very first recipient of this scholarship.

"In August, I moved to Brentwood, Maryland, and began my doctoral study. This was the academic program I enjoyed more than any other, as I had more freedom to pursue my own interests." Sally stayed in Maryland for most of the next three years, where she had secured a small basement apartment that allowed cats and was near a church. During her third year, she joined the Air Force Reserves and became a flight nurse. Although she planned to stay for only three years, she eventually completed twenty-four years in the Air Force Reserves.

"I was promised that I would be promoted to major when I completed flight school and qualified as a flight nurse," Sally recalls. "Fortunately, this was another idle recruiter promise; otherwise my military career would have been short. There was only one slot for a major in the 756th Reserve Unit, and I was outranked for that."

Sally did achieve the rank of captain. "When we landed on naval bases, announcing, 'Captain Nicholson wants transportation' brought quick results. Our unit required at least one training flight per month. These provided extra money, which was very welcome when I was a student at the University of Maryland."

While working at Children's Medical Center, Donna enrolled part time at Texas Woman's University in the psychiatric and mental-health nursing master's program with a subspecialty in pediatrics. While enrolled in the program, she was inducted into the Beta Beta Chapter of Sigma Theta Tau, an honorary nursing sorority, and she also established and moderated mothers' support groups on two of the inpatient floors at Children's Medical Center. These groups were so popular that she soon needed another graduate student to assist.

"With time and observation I became keenly aware of the opportunity and value of art as an innate and natural means of communication for all children, sick and well," Donna says. Thus she embarked on a research study, "Identification of Children's Fears through Their Drawings and Dialogue," which morphed into her master's thesis in 1972. Her research led to invitations to lead workshops and to give presentations for school and day-care teachers and professional nurses, including the pediatric nursing staff at Bellevue Hospital in New York City, where she presented art as a tool of identification, intervention, and therapy.

After completing her degree, she resigned from Children's Medical Center. She intended to take some time off, but just before the school year began, the principal of Highland Park High School asked Donna to consider being the school nurse. Both of Donna's daughters attended the school, which was only a few blocks from their home.

"I accepted with the caveat that it was temporary until they could find a full-time nurse," Donna says. "I stayed for the entire school year, and the graduating class asked me to chaperone their graduation lake party with another nurse who also had a daughter at the school. Happily, there were no emergencies for the students that day. Today, I would never take on that responsibility."

The next year Texas Woman's University needed to fill a faculty position in the undergraduate program. Donna's interview with the dean was short. "I accepted the position that day."

Donna enjoyed teaching classes at Texas Woman's University and was asked to author a chapter on therapeutic intervention with children through art. [9]

Around this time educational institutions were moving toward requiring doctoral degrees for faculty, and the master's-prepared faculty members at Texas Woman's University were requested to comply. However, they could not seek a doctorate from a school in the Texas University system if their master's degree was from a school in the same system.

"Conveniently, Southern Methodist University, a private university in Dallas, was only a mile from our home, and they were initiating a PhD program in medical anthropology chaired by Dr. Barbara Anderson from Berkeley. She was a gerontologist and author of

The Aging Game: Success, Sanity and Sex after 60, published by McGraw-Hill in 1979." Donna entered the program part time. "Our class was small, composed of two nurses and a vocational therapist, Peace Corp worker, nutritionist, social worker, and a few others with various backgrounds."

During this course of study Donna developed a pediatric cardiac questionnaire for a research project being conducted in a south Texas children's heart hospital serving a large population of Hispanic Americans. Dr. Anderson and doctoral student Nancy Hazam were the investigators.

Dallas was becoming a global city with many ethnic groups, the latest being Vietnamese, Cambodians, Chinese, Koreans, Iranians, and a smaller contingent of Ethiopians and Nigerians. Children's Medical Center was treating many more patients of different nationalities. These new cultural groups provided a laboratory of study, and the concept of ethnocentrism and the Western Medical Model of beliefs and delivery systems became prominent and fertile topics.

One summer while she was in the PhD program, Donna attended Southern Methodist University's Fort Burgwin Field School in Taos, New Mexico. The professor was Dr. Nancy Scheper-Hughes from Southern Methodist University, who later returned to the University of California-Berkeley, her alma mater. "Taos Pueblo has been continuously occupied for centuries, and that summer was my first exposure to an Indian population, their belief systems, and their cultural customs."

In April of 1981, Donna, three other doctoral candidates, and their professor, Dr. Anderson, traveled to the University of Edinburgh, Scotland, to make presentations at the Forty-First Annual Meeting of the Society for Applied Anthropology. Applied anthropology focuses on practicing anthropology in fields pertaining to health, education, communities, and organizations. Donna's presentation, "The

Dilemma of the Dual Professional (Nurse/Anthropologist) in Specific Case Contexts," amplified the unique melding of nursing and applied anthropology.

Dr. Madeleine Leininger, RN, championed the merging of applied anthropology and nursing. She founded the transcultural nursing movement as well as the *Journal of Transcultural Nursing* and the Transcultural Nursing Society. Her Cultural Care Theory advanced nursing theory by describing the theoretical concept of "culturally congruent care."

For Donna's dissertation in medical anthropology, she planned to study body image in Caucasian, Black, and Hispanic boys, ages eight to nine, in an orthopedic children's hospital. "I was disappointed to find out the hospital review committee considered the study 'politically incorrect' because it might cause a major donor to withdraw monetary support," Donna says.

She wrote a new dissertation proposal in which she would examine nursing-care delivery systems and the Children's Medical Center decision to consider transitioning from a team-nursing model to a primary-care nursing model. She was certain it would be accepted since she was asked to consider conducting this study by Children's Medical Center and was awarded a monetary scholarship from Southern Methodist University to do so. In 1986 she defended her dissertation, "Process, Patterns and Paradox in Primary Nursing: A Case Study of Planned Change in a Children's Hospital," and graduated from Southern Methodist University.

After getting her doctorate degree, Donna directed her efforts toward fundraising. Brantley and Donna had bought a home in Santa Fe, New Mexico, where they went for a few days each month and all summer. "While in northern New Mexico I became familiar with a particular Native American pueblo and some of its inhabitants," she says. "The tragic car wreck that took the lives of three young college freshman boys from this pueblo led me to promote awareness and monetary support to address substance abuse as well as other health issues that are prevalent in the Indian population."

In the summer of 1971, Bette was transferred to the Veterans Administration Medical Center in Washington, DC, to be one of the first five clinical nurse specialists (CNSs) introduced into the facility. The specialties for these advanced practice nurses were cardiovascular, medical, pulmonary, and psychiatry, as well as Bette's specialty of consultation-liaison psychiatry.

The chief of nursing service, Ms. Suzanne Dziak, did not announce their arrival to other chiefs of services but arranged with the hospital director and head nurses for the CNSs to quietly appear on the units, wearing white lab coats over street clothes, which was new at that time. These new nurses were connected to the chief of nursing service through a direct clinical line.

"The medical staff was puzzled about these nurses who wore lab coats like physicians," Bette recalls. "It quickly became apparent that each of us was in demand by nurses for our nursing specialties, but also from other members of the health-care team. We wrote on patients' progress notes instead of separate nurses' notes—another first for our hospital."

The CNSs developed job descriptions that defined each CNS specialty within a broad framework. As more CNSs were hired throughout the VA system, they helped the VA Central Office write a national job description that was very similar to what they wrote for the hospital. "We were happy and excited to be part of this change in nursing practice, even with inevitable adjustments," Bette says.

As the psychiatric-liaison clinical nurse specialist, Bette functioned independently and collaboratively with all staff on the medical and surgical inpatient units and with members of the psychiatric consultation service. She was responsible and accountable for her own caseload of patients during their hospitalization and follow-up.

"Requests for my intervention or supportive psychotherapy emanated from my clinical expertise, not authority from nursing administration," Bette remembers. "Any staff member in the medical center could request my help for patients, family members, or others without fear of their performance being evaluated or judged. Since nurses are generally perceived as helpful, patients responded positively when I introduced myself as a mental health nurse and asked how they were doing."

Bette's role was to assess patients and assist them in understanding and adapting to a physical illness—whether it was a new diagnosis, a recurrence, or a chronic disease—and when appropriate recommend formal psychiatric consultation. "Referrals included patients dealing with amputation, effects of a stroke, cancer, heart disease, HIV/AIDS, issues of body disturbance, loss, grief, death and dying, and sexual trauma," Bette says.

Bette became and remained the only nurse member of the medical center's Psychiatric Consultation Service until she retired in the year 2000. An early assignment for this new group of CNSs was to give a program on discharge planning as the nursing service's first program to receive continuing education units.

"I met weekly with the chief of the service, Dr. Paul D. Barnes, and in conferences with the psychiatric consultation team—composed of residents and medical students—to integrate our work with patients and staff. This team support was invaluable for maintaining high quality of care, preventing burnout, and creating an enjoyable work environment."

Bette found it especially satisfying to act as a preceptor/mentor for graduate students during their clinical specialization practicum in psychiatric consultation liaison nursing. "I was appointed to the position of adjunct assistant professor in the Catholic University of America's School of Nursing, Washington, DC, via the recommendation of the dean, Sister Rosemary Donley, PhD. It was heartening to work with her as well as with students over the years."

In March, 1978, Bette was among the first group of nurses, 101 in total, to be certified as specialists (CS) in psychiatric and mental health nursing by the ANA Division on Psychiatric and Mental Health Nursing Practice Certification Board. Among the requirements for certification were holding a master's or higher degree in nursing, several years of experience with clinical supervision, submission of a case study, and a written examination. "I could now sign my name followed by MSN, RN, and CS. I contributed to the next certification exam as an item writer and was a reader/evaluator of written case documentation for the ANA certification examination in the spring of 1981. Around this time, it also was gratifying to learn that I had been inducted, as a charter member, into the Delta Mu Chapter of the Sigma Theta Tau International Honor Society of Nursing, Yale University School of Nursing."

In 1980, Bette became a charter member of the Nurses Organization of Veterans Affairs (NOVA), a professional organization made up of registered nurses employed by the US Department of Veterans Affairs (DVA). The organization was formed after widespread discontent led to many nurses leaving the profession. The ensuing shortage of registered nurses reached crisis proportions in the VA health-care system in the fall of 1980. VA nurses were particularly unhappy when Congress passed a law that ensured competitive pay for VA physicians without any change in nurses' salaries or any input from VA nurses.

Registered nurses at the Hines VA Medical Center in Illinois spearheaded the formation of a nationwide professional organization that would ensure that a significant bill involving VA nurses and veteran health care would never again be presented and debated in Congress without the voice of VA nurses.

Motivated by NOVA president Elaine Lloyd and legislative director Noreen Sommer, both from the Palo Alto VA Medical Center in California, Bette became founding president of a NOVA chapter at the Washington, DC, VA Medical Center. This chapter was crucial because of the access it would have to Capitol Hill.

"My naïve and unanticipated entry into the political arena and leadership in a national nurses organization was something I had not yearned for, but embraced," Bette recalls. "Noreen, bright and fun-loving, became my mentor, introducing me to the dance of legislation. NOVA gave me the means to act on all that I had learned and was about to learn."

Encouraged by her colleagues' enthusiasm and friendship, Bette was elected to NOVA's National Board of Directors in 1988. "At my first board meeting I was assigned to be chairman of NOVA's national annual meeting program for 1989," Bette recalls. "I immediately knew whom to contact to speak—two national nursing leaders I knew while at Yale as well as the assistant chief medical director for nursing programs at the DVA, Vernice Ferguson."

The program for the 1989 meeting, VA Nursing: The Challenge in a Changing Environment, drew record attendance. Ferguson was the keynote speaker. Dr. Angela McBride, president of Sigma Theta Tau International, presented "Orchestrating a Career in Nursing," and Dr. Dumas, president of the American Academy of Nursing, addressed "Strategies for Nursing in Influencing Health Policy." A few years later, in 1993, Bette called on Donna Diers, Dean of Yale from 1972 to 1985, to give the keynote address, "Influencing Health Care Policy." She emphasized that the DVA was positioned to be part of the solution to universal health care and described the DVA nursing system as a recognizable political force.

In 1988, Bette also became a member of the legislative committee, and her national leadership role for NOVA began. In 1990, she became the organization's legislative director, and Noreen was president. Months of legislative work led to the passage of the VA Nurse Pay Act of 1990, establishing a pay system intended to make VA hospital pay competitive with that of other facilities in their local market.

Bette speaking at the ANA nursing rally on Capitol Hill in 1992.

The law designated the US Bureau of Labor to determine VA nurse pay, but since it had no salary data for nurses, staff from the VA Central Office drew up policies and regulations. Soon after the law's implementation in 1991, problems arose that were related to the new pay-grade structure, and the process used to survey local pay resulted in pay compression for many upper-grade VA nurses.

In 1992, Bette became president of NOVA and spoke to the Senate and House VA Committees in support of policy changes and amendments to the VA Nurse Pay Act of 1990, which were also supported by the ANA and the Veterans Service Organizations. In the final days of the 102nd Congress, the Veterans Health Care Act of 1992 passed. This added a fifth grade to the nurse pay-grade schedule, which benefitted nurses in administration and took a first step toward correcting problems.[10] "The passage of the Veterans Health Care Act of 1992 showed that nurse leaders could change health and public policy that benefitted the nursing profession," Bette says.

During Bette's time with NOVA, in particular her two years as president (1992–1994), she authored and presented numerous NOVA testimonies before the DVA and the US Senate and House VA Committees. Topics included legislation addressing the future of the VA health-care system, the role of the VA and of nurses in national health-care reform (President Clinton's American Health Security Act of 1993), women's health care, nurse pay, federal funding for nursing education, research and practice, expansion of various health-care programs, and the VA's flexibility in meeting medical workforce needs.

"It was challenging, exhilarating, and rewarding," Bette says. "I worked with some of the best nurses and people in the nation and hobnobbed with the mighty on Capitol Hill, in the White House, and at the DVA and ANA on behalf of a political voice for VA nurses and all nurses. Of course I thoroughly enjoyed the receptions, events, and other activities taking place. Being part of these important events enabled me to contribute to health care on a national level."

Bette with Representative Sonny (G. V.) Montgomery, chairman of the House Veterans Committee; Elaine Lloyd, president of NOVA; and Noreen Sommer, legislative director of NOVA.

For example, Bette was a spokesperson at the Lamplight Rally for Health Care Reform on Capitol Hill during National Nurses Week in 1992. This was nursing's first rally on Capitol Hill, sponsored by the ANA to demonstrate nursing's unified commitment to health care. Representing NOVA, she was among more than 150 nurses who attended a Briefing for the President's Task Force on National Health Care Reform and a reception held in the White House Rose Garden with President Clinton in May, 1993. During the selection process for a new Veterans Health Administration Chief of Patient Care Services, Bette participated as the nurse member of the DVA's interview panel from December, 1995, to January, 1996.

In 1997, NOVA presented Bette with the Barbara Chambers Award for her leadership and outstanding contributions to NOVA. Chambers was the founding president of NOVA in 1980. Bette was cited for her work in enhancing the political power of VA professional nursing, making it a visible and interactive force in shaping Department of Veterans Affairs health-care policies and nursing's role in that health care.

From 1971 to 2000, Bette practiced as a CNS at the Washington, DC, VA Medical Center. This position kept her at the forefront of direct care. "Nurses before me pursued ways and means to improve nursing education and advanced practice, making it possible for nurses to remain in the clinical area."

After obtaining her PhD in human development from the University of Maryland in 1973, Sally returned to her position at the UNC School of Nursing. "Now I had responsibility for developing the graduate major in pediatric nursing," Sally says. She was tenured as an assistant professor and very busy with her teaching and reserve duties, the latter of which required that she drive to Andrews Air Force Base in Maryland one weekend each month as well as take some trips for training flights.

Sally became chief nurse of the Reserve Unit at Andrews Air Force Base soon after Bette transferred there in the summer of 1971. For the next five years, they enjoyed working together as flight nurses in the aeromedical evacuation unit. "At every monthly training drill, Sally would bring cookies and cakes for all to enjoy, something dearly appreciated and remembered—in awe—whenever Sally is mentioned by unit members," Bette recalls.

In 1972 and 1973, Sally flew with physicians from the UNC Medical School to Fayetteville and then to Wilmington one day per week to teach public health nurses techniques for physical examination of children. "I loved flying on those small planes," she remembers.

She applied for a promotion to associate professor at the School of Nursing. "When this did not happen, I began looking for another position, as my doctorate was completed," she recalls. "I considered positions at the University of South Carolina and the University of North Carolina at Charlotte."

In 1974, Sally accepted a position at the UNC Charlotte School of Nursing as an associate professor, fulfilling a need for their public health program. She and the dean were the only doctoral-prepared nurses on the faculty. The dean resigned the next year, and when the new dean was hired, Sally became assistant to the dean, a position she held until 1983. "I continued to teach a growth-and-development course and a nursing research course to mostly undergraduate nursing students and taught community health nursing as part of a team."

In 1978, a faculty team developed the Pathways Program for registered nurses to earn baccalaureate degrees. Two years later, Sally joined this team and continued to be a member for the remainder of her time at UNC Charlotte. Sally was promoted to professor of nursing in 1977.

In 1976, Sally transferred from the Air Force Reserve to the North Carolina Air National Guard as part of the 156th Aero Medical Unit. "In this position, I had the opportunity to participate in two assignments, during which I flew with active duty Aero Medical Evacuation units in the United States and Germany that were transporting patients."

She went on to become the first woman in the North Carolina Air National Guard to achieve the rank of lieutenant colonel. Sally participated in moving simulated patients around Germany and to England in the Exercise Reforger. This exercise was conducted annually during the Cold War to make sure that NATO could quickly deploy forces to West Germany if there were to be a conflict with the Warsaw Pact.

From January to June, 1985, Sally was the visiting professor of nursing at the University of Northern Colorado, where she taught community nursing and conducted clinical supervision in psychiatric nursing. During this time she wrote a chapter on adolescent development for the Pediatric Nursing Test in 1978 and later revised it in 1985.

Sally retired as a lieutenant colonel from the air force on December 31, 1991, and in 1993 she also retired from UNC Charlotte, becoming professor emerita. She then accepted the position of professor of community health nursing at Gardner-Webb University in Boiling Springs, North Carolina, from which she retired in August, 1993. She helped the nursing program at Gardner-Webb achieve accreditation and guided development of their Sigma Theta Tau Chapter.

Sally is an ordained minister in the Brigade of Light Church. "I also write poetry, some of which has been published. Dogs and cats have been very important to my life as well as growing plants, orchids, and vegetables."

Geri, after attending a graduation at Staten Island Community College.

By 1968, Uncle Sam was paying for nurses with a bachelor of science degree to return to a university for a master of education. Geri took advantage of this program and attended the New York University School of Education as a full-time graduate student from 1968 to 1970.

Her first teaching position was with City University at Staten Island Community College during the first year of a new policy that assured students who graduated from a New York City high school entrance to one of the colleges of City University.

"Soon it became clear to me that I was a pretty good classroom professor but not so good at faculty-staff meetings," Geri remembers. "Too much of these meetings seemed to be 'much ado about nothing.'"

So Geri moved away from formal education to more community-related positions. She was a consultant for Home Health Agencies with Blue Cross Blue Shield and then was a consultant with the New York State Department of Health for Skilled Nursing Facilities.

Then in 1986, Geri and Bob returned to Chapel Hill after Bob retired from banking. "Chapel Hill was a special place to live in 1951 and remains so today," Geri says.

In Chapel Hill, Bob went to graduate school, and Geri joined the Home Health Agency as a part-time staff member. She made home visits, chiefly to geriatric patients. After his graduation, Bob became a consultant with the US Agency for International Development, and Geri continued her nursing position with the Home Health Agency part time. "This allowed me

Geri and her husband, Bob.

to continue my international travel to visit Bob as he worked in India, Guatemala, Fiji, Egypt, Australia, and various South Pacific Islands."

Geri decided to retire after the Chapel Hill Home Health Agency was sold to a proprietary for-profit agency. After the events of 9/11 left the World Trade Center demolished, it was time for Bob to leave the international life. "Having had an office on the forty-ninth floor of one of the towers while with the New York State Department of Health, the World Trade Center had been a real part of our lives," Geri says.

---

[8] D. Diers, R.L. Schmidt, M.A. McBride, and B.L. Davis. 1972. The Effect of Nursing Interaction on Patients in Pain. *Nursing Research*, 21: 419-428.

[9] D. B. Booe. (1980). Therapeutic Intervention with Children through Art. In *Community Mental Health Nursing: An Ecological Perspective*, edited by Jeanette Lancaster, 179-199, Mosby Co.

[10] Noreen Sommer and Bette Davis contributed an account of this legislation in the following publication: D.J. Mason, S. Talbott, and J. Leavitt. 1993. *Policy and Politics for Nurses: Action and Change in the Workplace, Government, Organizations and Community.* Second Edition. Philadelphia: W.B. Saunders Company.

11

Celebrating Fifty
Years and Beyond

As part of their forty-fifth reunion, the class of 1955 attended a tea reception, where they met the school's new dean, Linda Cronenwett. Pictured are Winnie, Joy, Geri, Dean Cronenwett, Bette, Mary, Janet, and Martha.

The year 2000 marked the fiftieth anniversary of the School of Nursing. In May of that year, members of the nursing class gathered for the General Alumni Association Class of 1955 Forty-Fifth Reunion. They met on Friday for lunch at Top of the Hill restaurant, and later joined the North Carolina barbecue event on the lawn of The Carolina Inn. On Saturday, they attended a special tea reception at The Carolina Inn to meet the new dean of the School of Nursing, Linda Cronenwett.

"We were enthralled by her and delighted that she specifically wanted to meet with us," Bette says. Martha wrote, "Isn't our new dean approachable as well as lovely. We all are blessed."

Celebration activities for their forty-fifth class reunion and the school's fiftieth year started on Friday, November 10, with a black-tie evening of dinner and fifties swing dancing at The Carolina Club. "We had a fabulous time reconnecting and sharing memories with class-mates, other alumni, and original faculty members Ms. Gifford and Ms. Dalrymple," Bette says.

The School of Nursing celebrated its fiftieth anniversary with a black-tie gala. Geri and Bob, Gwen and Dean, and Martha and Bob are pictured.

On Saturday, they enjoyed a display of nursing memorabilia from the school's early days, primarily on loan from Winnie. "The first class of UNC graduates developed a unique bond," Winnie says. "At each class reunion, we seemed able to pick up as if there were no intervening years since we last met. I was particularly pleased to be able to contribute a uniform, cape, original textbooks, acceptance letter, rules and regulations, and many more papers to the nursing archives."

"By 2002, the nursing school was expanding, and our class participated in the Carolina First Campaign for the School of Nursing by sponsoring funding for the Alumni Welcome Center and Alumni Conference Room, something that could be enjoyed by all who came to the School of Nursing," Janet recalls.

Members of the class of 1955 gave $60,400 through a five-year pledge to the campaign, with 100 percent of the class contributing. Being in the first class was unique, and they were proud of their legacy. "This was our way of welcoming all alumni who follow in our footsteps," Bette says. The school recognized the gift by placing a permanent donor-recognition plaque, listing all seventeen graduates of the first class, on the wall inside the Alumni Conference Room next to the painting of Smith Dormitory.

To celebrate their contribution, twelve members of the class met on November 9, 2002, to present the class of 1955 gift to Dean Cronenwett. They selected the Aurora Restaurant for dinner because it was formerly The Pines Restaurant, owned by Janet's parents and one of their favorite places to eat.

In November, 2002, class members gathered at the Aurora Restaurant to present their gift to Dean Cronenwett. Pictured are Bette, Rae, Gwen, Gloria, Joy, Geri, Winnie, Pat, Janet, Mary, Martha, Dean Cronenwett, and Louise.

Rae's husband and painter, Ed Starnes, shared the news that he would create a commemorative watercolor painting to hang in the new building. The members of the class of 1955, Dean Cronenwett, and Norma Hawthorne and Anne Webb from the school's Office of Advancement made this collective effort possible. The class gathered for a reception on May 6, 2004, to honor Rae and Ed's donation of two original watercolor paintings to hang in Carrington Hall and the new building addition.

They hovered over him while he signed limited-edition prints for every class member. The painting of Smith Building on main campus, called *The Beginning*, was to hang in the Alumni Conference Room and was reproduced only for members of the class of 1955. "This

University Day by Ed Starnes

painting of our freshman-year dormitory reminds us of many memories," Bette says. "It is a reminder of relationships, student life, and memories, uniquely ours, formed while we lived there."

The painting *University Day* captured the graduates by the Old Well preparing for the processional to Kenan Stadium. It hangs in the new addition to Carrington Hall as a tribute to the people and landmarks that make UNC such a special place. Rae and Ed donated five hundred signed prints of *University Day* as incentives for $200 gifts to the School of Nursing Building Fund. "This painting serves to remind me each day of the poignant memories of my beloved Chapel Hill—my school and my home," Janet says.

The class of 1955 fiftieth reunion in 2005 proved to be a grand occasion that was in a class all its own. "As the first class of nursing, we were recognized and introduced at various functions over the course of several days," recalls Janet. "The entire weekend was filled with activities, and we were extremely honored to be in attendance and most appreciative of all our recognition. Most of all, we were thankful to be there to celebrate fifty years—together."

Fifty years after they graduated, the School of Nursing class of 1955 led the graduation processional on commencement day.

The reunion took place on commencement weekend and began with the General Alumni Association's Old Students Club Luncheon on Friday, May 13, at George Watts Hill Alumni Center. "We were inducted into the club, and each member received a certificate and a commemorative medallion. That evening we met at the Friday Frolic event for food and dancing in the students' new dining hall," Bette recalls.

The class of 1955 at the Friday Frolic, celebrating their fiftieth
reunion in 2005. Seated: Winnie, Gloria, Gwen, and Sally.
Standing: Louise, Geri, Bette, Donna, Joy, Janet, and Rae.

On commencement day, representatives from Carolina's class of 1955 joined the academic processional that precedes the undergraduates. The School of Nursing's first graduating class, in their Carolina-blue gowns, led the processional into Kenan Stadium proudly wearing the medallions and happily waving. "This was an even more special occasion for me, as my granddaughter Jennifer was also graduating from the Kenan Flagler School of Business," Janet says.

In the afternoon, the UNC School of Nursing held its commencement for the class of 2005 in Carmichael Auditorium. Dean Cronenwett noted the celebration of their fiftieth anniversary of graduation from Carolina and introduced each graduate of the first nursing class as they walked across the stage. "We looked at the large group of current graduates and realized we had come a long way from the original seventeen," Janet says. "What a legacy we had created."

Bette spoke on behalf of the class, congratulating and welcoming the graduates as new alumni to the school's alumni association. "We were honored and appreciative to participate in the commencement program," she says. "This was truly special."

The busy day continued as they rushed to attend the Carolina Class of 1955 Fiftieth Reunion Banquet at The Carolina Inn. Events included cocktails, a class photo, dinner, and an entertainment program designed to remind the class of 1955 of who they were fifty years ago. "As usual, we managed to get two tables close together for our group," Bette says. "Albert Long, master of ceremonies, asked me to speak for three minutes. I gave a brief overview of our arrival on campus to refresh memories of twenty-seven freshman girls entering a largely boys' school. A half century later, there were over 6,600 alumni in the School of Nursing. I got laughter when I ended with an anecdote about learning to cope when least expected, the one mentioned in chapter 3 about not forgetting the word 'regurgitate.'"

In 1974, Joy had moved to New Orleans, where dancing in the street was commonplace. She brought this practice to Chapel Hill's famous Franklin Street during the fiftieth class reunion. "While some of my classmates and I were passing through a group of celebrating students, a steel band was playing New Orleans–style music. I instinctively swung my cane in the air and performed the 'Orleans Strut,' entertaining everyone and cheered on by my classmates as I danced across the street. We loved it—such fun being back in Chapel Hill together again. They will not let me forget about dancing in the street."

While preparing a memory book for the class of 1955's fiftieth reunion, Anne Webb from the School of Nursing Advancement Office requested anecdotal material that she could use. Some of the earlier written material sent to Janet and Joy was also sent to Anne for use in the memory book. This material later became a valuable resource for writing the class history, which began in earnest in 2010 as the class of 1955 prepared for their fifty-fifth reunion.

A later highlight came in 2008, when the Association of Nursing Students designed T-shirts with the class of 1955's photo and sold them as a fundraiser. "It was a huge hit," says Bette. "Obviously, our class was honored by this thoughtful action."

When the class of 1955 heard that Dean Cronenwett was retiring as dean, they decided that they must attend the reception to honor her on April 17, 2009. They first met for a class luncheon at the Weathervane in Chapel Hill, where they previewed the painting Ed Starnes had created, at their request, as a gift to Dean Cronenwett. The painting depicted the Quad, the dean's favorite scene on campus.

As the first president of the alumni association, Martha spoke at Dean Cronenwett's retirement reception.

Several hundred people attended Dean Cronenwett's reception at DuBose House. Anne remained hidden with the painting until Bette spoke. The moment that Bette said that she represented Ramelle Hylton Starnes and her husband, Edward Starnes, the dean's eyes lit up, indicating her surprise and joy when she guessed what was coming next.

Anne turned the painting around as Bette said, "We are so fortunate to have an artist in our family and in our school. This is an expression of our love for you." Rae and Ed were not able to make the event, but Bette recounted the day for them in a letter that portrayed how much everyone, especially the dean, was thrilled with the painting.

For the dean's memory book the class members made a card that they signed and that included the names of two deceased members: Virginia Edwards Coupe (1/9/95) and Sara Blaylock Flynn (10/9/08). The front cover held the following message:

Dean Linda Cronenwett

Our best wishes for you in your retirement.
Our hearts will always contain special loving memories of you.

The rich legacy of your deanship is a source of inspiration
for all and leaves a distinguished
period in the history of the UNC School of Nursing.
This is the work you were meant to do. Thank you.

The Class of 1955

The September 25, 2009, reception for Dean Kristen M. Swanson and the 2009 Alumni Awards brought the class together to welcome the new dean and to posthumously honor classmate Sara Blaylock Flynn as Alumna of the Year. Sara's husband and daughter, Linda Tara Flynn, received the award in her honor. The awards-committee chair, Nancy Smith, graciously presented the award and summarized Sara's lifetime of service in global nursing in the Middle East, Europe, and the United States.

"It was great being together again for a wonderful reception for the new dean, and to celebrate the 2009 alumni awardees, especially Sara," Bette says. After the event, Janet, Joy, Geri, and Bette joined Sara's husband and daughter at the hotel. "It was fun to remember Sara's spirit with her beautiful daughter and loving husband, as we certainly shall keep her in our hearts," Bette recalls. They celebrated into the night, sharing stories of their times together. "Consequently, Sara's daughter gained greater insight into her mother's college years," Janet says. "Just like her mother, she had come to know us not just as classmates, but as lifetime friends."

Sara Blaylock Flynn was posthumously honored as Alumna of the Year in 2009. Her husband and daughter, Linda Tara Flynn, received the award in her honor. Also pictured is Anne Webb.

The catchy theme for their fifty-fifth anniversary was "Fifty-Five for '55." UNC's General Alumni Association arranged a banquet at The Carolina Inn, where the class feasted and recalled, in jest, many memories associated with those girls in the School of Nursing. "It was quite pleasant and funny to be remembered by the other students on campus back in the early fifties," Bette recalls. "Ten of us and our spouses met again the next day at the Old Students Luncheon. It felt so good to be back home where it all started." They gave certificates of honorary membership in the UNC School of Nursing, class of 1955, to the husbands, who were considered very much part of their group. Later that day they met at Carrington Hall, where they also gave Anne an honorary class of 1955 membership certificate.

The class of 1955 met Dean Kristen Swanson during their fifty-fifth reunion. Seated: Pat, Janet. Sally, and Joy. Standing: Dean Swanson, Gloria, Mary, Bette, Donna, and Geri.

They also met with Dean Swanson, wearing the School of Nursing pins they received from Dean Kemble on graduation day on June 6, 1955. "It is a beautiful and meaningful pin, and this was an occasion to wear it proudly, for our new dean," Bette says.

Mary had to borrow her pin to wear on this special day. She had passed her pin on to one of her daughters, who graduated from the UNC Chapel Hill School of Nursing in 1984. The pin had Mary's initials and date of graduation as well as her daughter's initials and date of graduation on the back, and her daughter wore it while practicing at Duke University Medical Center in Durham, North Carolina.

Eleven members of the School of Nursing class of 1955 joined Anne Webb and Nancy Lamontagne at the UNC Old Students Luncheon in May, 2014.

That weekend Janet and Bette brought historical papers and some written ideas to revive interest in documenting their experiences. Donna came prepared with ideas and enthusiasm too, and along with Anne Webb and others, they restarted the process of writing their history. "As a group, we came to the realization that the years were going by rapidly," Janet says. They had lost two classmates since the last reunion, and aging health problems were common among others. "Each year has become more meaningful, and as a group, we decided to write about our journey together. So it had become a reality—to leave our legacy of all the memories shared as 'Chapel Hill's First Nightingales.'"

Anne and Nancy at the May 2014 Students Luncheon.

Class members met several more times to work on the book and receive updates on its progress. Eleven classmates, as well as Anne Webb and their editor, Nancy Lamontagne, gathered for the UNC Old Students Luncheon in May, 2014, and celebrated fifty-nine years since their graduation. The class felt especially happy that the goal of writing a book of their memoirs was in its final stage and decided a photo of Anne and Nancy to share with future readers was needed.

12

Reflections

The high standards imposed on the nursing students during their time in school helped shape the young nurses into citizens who made considerable contributions to nursing education and practice as well as to their families and communities.

The class of 1955 helped introduce a new approach to educating nurses in North Carolina, and in the process they learned how to proceed professionally even if not everyone they worked with was open to change. This experience and the leadership that dean Kemble showed in ensuring equality for the nursing school in the UNC Health Affairs Division gave the class of 1955 the confidence and skills they needed to take on leadership roles, whether or not they felt prepared for the new responsibilities.

Bette says that the challenges of being part of the first class of nurses prepared her for the projects she would later be a part of and influenced her career choices. "In various circumstances during the evolvement of my career, opportunities arose by happenstance, rather than design, for me to be a trailblazer or to be first. Whenever the next step presented itself, I simply took it." As a result, Bette forged new legislation and policies that advanced nursing and the quality of care in the VA health system.

Bette recalls that Dean Kemble taught them to think about the independent aspect of nursing practice, and she emphasized the importance of supporting nursing organizations because they worked to improve the nursing profession. "Throughout my career I have been intrigued about the role of nursing in health care. Perhaps the seed was planted in Dean Kemble's seminar, rooted during my role as head nurse, sprouted in graduate school, grew during my time as a clinical nurse specialist, and blossomed in my pivotal positions in the Nurses Organization of Veteran's Affairs (NOVA)."

Sara shaped and augmented nursing service in global nursing as she practiced in Saudi Arabia and Europe. "My experience was very rewarding, allowing me to implement nursing principles instilled in me by my UNC education," she says. The Bedouin women, babies, and children were greatly influenced by her teaching skills and "hands-on" nursing practice. Her influence expanded as the knowledge these mothers gained spread to their own villages. Sara's leadership and organizational skills were also apparent in the international health-consulting firm she and her husband formed in Belgium.

Donna looks back at the time the nursing students spent in public health departments as a harbinger of contemporary global health nursing as it is evolving on a worldwide basis, and as an inducement for her research to integrate cultural and art concepts applicable to nursing theory.

In retrospect, Donna says, "The four years in the nursing program at UNC were far more influential than I initially realized. Dean Kemble was the most influential change agent for nursing education and practice in North Carolina. The foundation of professional nursing with all accompanying expectations were carefully planned and executed by the dean and her faculty. For me, those values were instilled and reinforced with each passing year. The continuing thread throughout my career has been a quest for knowledge and an expansion of that foundation, which began at Chapel Hill. I am humbled, proud, and honored to be a graduate of the UNC School of Nursing, and being a member of the first class, the class of 1955, is a most treasured gift."

As the years have passed, nursing education has advanced with new degree programs, research, and development of expanded roles for professional nurses in a dynamic environment. Winnie, who taught in the early years of the LPN program in Craven County, North Carolina, says that the gift of education affected all aspects of her life. "Not only  was this true for us as the 'first UNC Nightingales,' but also for all those whom we taught. Education provided not only employment, but satisfaction, and it gave us needed information to care for our loved ones."

 Gloria helped develop an associate-degree nursing program in Lee County, North Carolina, and later directed the program. She gives credit to the School of Nursing for the good life she has enjoyed. "Our faculty held us to high standards of professional activity. They were wonderful mentors. I will always

be grateful to Ms. Ruth Boyles for coming to our door on that very hot day in August of 1951. Thanks, also, to my parents for sending me and supporting my educational desires."

Pat, who helped organize a two-year nursing program at Wayne Community College in Goldsboro, North Carolina, invested in the future of nursing by endowing scholarship funds. One is awarded annually to a second-year student attending the Wayne Community College Associates Degree in Nursing Program. Through a charitable gift annuity, the  other scholarship will provide financial aid to undergraduate students at the UNC School of Nursing in Chapel Hill.

 Sally forged new paths as the first woman in the North Carolina Air National Guard to achieve the rank of lieutenant colonel. "In the air force and as an educator, I have mentored colleagues as well as students and enjoyed watching them learn and grow personally as well as professionally," she says. "My undergraduate education at Carolina was always recognized as one of the best and was a door opener for my career choices."

Martha's education at the UNC School of Nursing prepared her to teach, interpret health, and explain disease in a doctor's office, classroom, and even at the bridge table. "Carolina gave me a sense of self that no one can take from me and pride of being part of a wonderful place and experience," she says.

In addition to her time in public health nursing and as a hospice nurse, Joy spent time as chair of the Charlotte Memorial Hospital Auxiliary's service committee and later became a published author. "I am grateful that I was accepted into the first class of nursing at UNC, as there were many candidates who applied," Joy says. "Throughout my life, with this education, I achieved success and satisfaction in my career, especially public health nursing and later as a hospice nurse. It has proven to give me skills to cope with difficult family illnesses, acute and chronic. I feel blessed to have been a nurse and able to care for my loved ones."

Gwen was the administrator of a 160-bed nursing home and says that her life has been a great ride because of her time and training at Chapel Hill. "We were taught many valuable lessons in addition to nursing, and it has all fallen into place through the years," she says. "Thank you, UNC School of Nursing and Dean Kemble and faculty."

Janet's journey as a registered nurse certainly proved to be gratifying one. She enjoyed being personally involved with her patients and their families. "I feel as though I touched many lives along the way, and more than a nurse, I was also a friend who cared. I am thankful that I had the educational skills and 'people skills' that helped me achieve my success."

Louise saw the field of public health nursing expand and mature during the time she practiced. "I count it a privilege to have been included in the first class entering the University of North Carolina School of Nursing," she says. "It was there I received a unique nursing educational experience, directed by a most forward and focused faculty in our own university setting."

Although Mary's professional tenure as a nurse was brief, she says that the nursing skills and values she learned at UNC were priceless as she experienced challenges of life, including chronic illness in her family.

Geri credits her experience at the School of Nursing with encouraging her to study and to think about subjects she had never previously considered. These skills prepared her to practice and teach in locations across the United States.

Rae was a chemistry teacher and then later helped start a nonprofit organization that provides volunteer support to patients with serious illnesses. She said that her time at the School of Nursing enriched her life by broadening her horizons, by instilling a sense of responsibility to the community, and by providing the best possible preparation for life's experiences.

Perhaps most of all, the class of 1955 values the friendships they gained by being a part of the first class. Gloria says that she cherishes the friendships that developed during their four years in nursing school. "These friendships become more important with each passing year," she says. Gwen echoes that sentiment, saying that the class friendships are invaluable. Janet says that the Chapel Hill Nightingales were prepared for their destination in life, and were successful, but their journey together has been their joy.

Picture Acknowledgements

Unless otherwise noted, photographs were provided by the UNC Chapel Hill School of Nursing or by members of the Class of 1955. The photo on page 165 is courtesy of Central Carolina Community College. Brian Strickland photographed the nursing cap pictured on the back cover.

19585571R00136

Made in the USA
Middletown, DE
26 April 2015